Handbook of Reading Activities

From Teacher to Parent to Child

[Carl F. Brown] Ph.D.
Mac Henry Brown, Ed.D.

Humanics Limited * Atlanta, Georgia

HUMANICS LIMITED
P.O. Box 7447
Atlanta, Georgia 30309

Library of Congress Card Catalog Number: 82-81897
PRINTED IN THE UNITED STATES OF AMERICA
ISBN 0-89334-036-7

Edited by Linda A. Robinson
Book and cover design by Laurie Svenkeson
Illustrations by Stacia Dillon & Laurie Svenkeson

Humanics Limited * Atlanta, Georgia

Table of Contents

Preface

The parent is the child's first and perhaps his best teacher. In the early life of the child, it is the parent who teaches the child how to walk, how to talk, how to dress himself, how to tie his shoes, and how to pick up his toys. The parent teaches the child practically everything he knows and does.

As the child gets older, he begins to go outside the home for some of his experiences and learning activities. Adults other than the parent begin to teach the child as he goes to play school, dancing lessons, music lessons, swimming lessons, summer day camp, scout meetings, the park, church school, and kindergarten. Now, the parent is not the teacher, but he gives support, encouragement, and reinforcement for the child's learning activities. And parents continue to play an active and important role in the child's learning experiences. They help their children learn the Scout oath, memorize a part for a play, practice a swimming stroke or dance steps for a recital, and practice manuscript writing. They support the work of other adults who are teaching their child.

As the child goes to school, it is the professional teacher who does the formal teaching. The parent, however, who has always participated in the child's learning, still has a role to play. There is no reason to suggest that at this most important period in the child's life the parent should suddenly withdraw from the teaching-learning process and "leave it to the teacher who is paid to do the teaching". The parent can *still* supplement the work of the teacher. He can reinforce the learning which takes place in school and give the child added practice in the skills which the child is trying to master.

Most parents realize that all children can benefit from individual help in learning to read. Teaching reading is very complex and specialized, however, and most parents don't know how to teach reading. Many, many parents are in fact frustrated because they do not know what to do to help their children learn to read. Further, they feel that even if they did know *what* to do, they do not have the *materials* to do it with! Concerned parents quite naturally turn to the teacher to find out what they can do to help their children with reading.

Teachers have recognized that many parents could provide help and practice in specific skill areas if they knew what to do and if they had the appropriate materials. But teachers have also been frustrated when parents ask, "How can I help my child with reading?" Until now, teachers have not had written explanations, suggestions, and exercises that are specifically designed to be shared with parents who wish to work with their children at home.

This manual supplies just such materials. Now, when the parent asks what he can do to help his child with reading, the teacher has the answer. The teacher suggests to the parent the skills in which the student needs practice and individual help. The teacher reproduces the appropriate lessons from HANDBOOK OF READING ACTIVITIES and gives them to the parent to use at home. The parent will find that the carefully organized and easy-to-do exercises and activities provide meaningful learning experiences for the child.

HANDBOOK OF READING ACTIVITIES is not tied to any reading series but contains exercises in the major reading skills taught in the primary grades. The exercises are useful in either developmental or remedial reading. The exercises are clearly written and easy for the parent to use.

With the help of HANDBOOK OF READING ACTIVITIES the teacher finds some much-needed help and the teacher and parent can work together to help the child improve his reading skills. The result is a stronger reading program. And the ultimate beneficiary is the child.

To the Teacher:

As you teach the various specific reading skills, you are aware that children react differently to instruction. Some children acquire the skills being taught very quickly and easily. Other children need further explanations, more illustrations, repetitive practice, and individual attention. Schools are so organized that a teacher's best efforts are often insufficient to provide the individual attention needed by all students. In many cases the child's parent can provide the help the individual child needs. There are parents, of course, who cannot and will not help their children with school work at home. Many others, however, frequently ask teachers to tell them what they can do at home to help the child. The willing parent who understands the skill to be taught and the methods to be used, and who has the appropriate materials, can provide the needed individual help. This book provides you with exercises you can give the parent to use with his child at home to reinforce your instructon in school.

This manual provides exercises on many of the major reading skills taught in the primary grades. The lessons are not tied to any single reading series but would be useful for any child in a developmental or remedial reading program who is still learning the basic skills.

Let's assume that in a conference with Johnny's mother, you point out that you are now working on the recognition of "letter names". Many children have responded well to your lessons. Some other children, including Johnny, need more practice with this skill. Using the table of contents, you quickly find the exercises that will be helpful to Johnny. You duplicate a copy of the appropriate lessons on "letter names" for the mother to use at home. You may wish to go over the introduction to the section with the parent and see that she understands how to use the lessons. The parent leaves with carefully organized and easy-to-do exercises she can use with the child at home. Any time a child needs special help and practice you may send the parent exercises to use at home so that the child gets help with a skill he needs to master. You are still the person who teaches the skills in your regular program, but the parent can reinforce your work by providing the individual help and practice needed by the child.

This cooperation between the parent and the teacher brings about a better total reading program. It gives the teacher some much-needed help and it reduces reading retardation by providing more individulal attention for the child.

To the Parent:

The school uses a reading program which teaches your child the needed reading skills. These skills are presented over a period of years. Children who fail to learn the skills when they are presented often get into trouble in reading. But all children do not respond in the same way when the teacher teaches a specific skill. Some children master one skill quickly and easily but need help on another. Some children have trouble learning most of the skills. The teacher can not always find time to give each child just the individual help he needs in order to learn a skill. Sometimes a child needs another explanation, more examples, or more practice before he can master the skill. Here is where the parent can play an important role in the child's reading program.

Before the child started to school, you helped him in almost all of his learning situations. You helped your child learn how to walk, talk, eat, dress himself, and tie his shoes. You helped others teach your child how to dance and swim. You helped your child learn the Scout oath, and memorize a part for a play, and learn to write the alphabet and his name. Now that your child is in school, you sometimes feel inadequate. Some parents are heard to say, "I am not a teacher, and I certainly don't know how to teach reading." Others say that they feel that the teaching should be "left to the teachers who are trained and paid to do the teaching." But obviously, you who have always helped your child in learning situations can still supplement the work of the teacher. You can reinforce the learning which takes place at school and give your child added practice with the skills he is trying to master. In this way you can help prevent reading difficulties for your child and help him become a good reader.

Many parents know that they could help their child if they knew what to do and if they had the appropriate materials with which to do it. HANDBOOK OF READING ACTIVITIES gives you the exercises you can use to help your child with specific reading skills. Your child's teacher will give you the exercises he/she knows will be helpful to your child. The material is carefully planned and easy to follow. The exercises require only a few minutes a day. You can now be of great help to your child and to his reading teacher as you work together to help the child become a good reader.

Here are some "Tips on Teaching" which will help you work well with your child.

1. Be confident. Expect the child to learn the skill you're working on.
2. Help your child to be confident and believe "I can do it".
3. Help your child feel secure, so that when things go wrong he won't feel that he's a failure.
4. Never miss a chance to praise your child for doing a good job.
5. Point out to the child what he's learned and the progress he's made.
6. Don't let your child think of the lessons as punishment.
7. Work with your child at a time that doesn't interfere with his favorite TV show or other activities he enjoys.

8. *Don't make a learning period too long. If the child begins to tire, it's time to stop.*
9. *Help your child to feel successful. Every session should end on a pleasant note.*
10. *Give your child your undivided attention during your time with him.*
11. *Try to enjoy every session with your child. He is more likely to enjoy it!*
12. *Help your child understand the reason for each exercise and try to motivate him to do well.*

Reading Readiness

To the Parent:

All a child's experiences contribute favorably or unfavorably to his learning to read. A proper balance of physical, intellectual, environmental, and emotional factors makes it easy and pleasurable for a child to learn to read. Children with the proper balance are said to be "ready" to read. An improper balance of readiness factors interferes with learning to read. Those children who are deficient in one or more readiness factors are said to be "unready" to read. Reading readiness programs are designed to help those children get ready to learn to read.

When a child is "ready" and wants to learn to read, the teacher says he is motivated. Motivation stems from early life experiences. The child learns that reading is important when there are lots of books and magazines in his house, when the child is read to and sees other people reading, and when he goes to the library and finds new and exciting books that appeal to him. The child learns that words tell us things we need to know. Pointing out words on stop signs, store signs, and words representing favorite things like ice cream, helps the child learn that words have meanings and contributes to his motivation to learn to read.

Before a child can learn to read, however, he needs specific skills, as well as readiness and motivation. Some of the reading readiness skills may be taught directly to children. Among these are visual discrimination and auditory discrimination.

Visual discrimination means that the child has good eyesight and can see likenesses and differences in letter form and word form. Every child's eyes should be checked to see that he has good eyesight. Seeing small details at a glance is a must for reading. Seeing such differences as those between E and F and q and p is not easy and most children need specific practice. The visual discrimination activities in this book are designed to give the child practice in recognizing likenesses and differences in letters and words, and in looking for details.

Auditory discrimination means that the child can hear well and has learned how to hear the different sounds which make up words. Every child's hearing should be checked to be sure he can hear well. Hearing how words are made up of different sounds and hearing which sounds come at the beginning, in the middle, or at the end of a word is a skill children need to acquire as they learn to read. The auditory discrimination activities in this book will teach your child to hear how sounds are alike and different and to match sounds to the letters which represent them.

Reading readiness programs help children recognize letters, call letter names instantly, and know which sounds the letters represent. The exercises in this book on letters will help your child learn the letters, write the letters, and know the sounds which the letters represent.

The willing parent can help his child with visual and auditory readiness by following the teacher's suggestions. It is most important that the child have a lot of practice in using his eyes for small details, in listening for sounds in words, and in writing letters and matching sounds to letters.

Visual
Discrimination

1

Purpose: To help the child see how things are alike and how they are different.

Directions: Ask the child to draw a line connecting the pictures that are exactly alike.

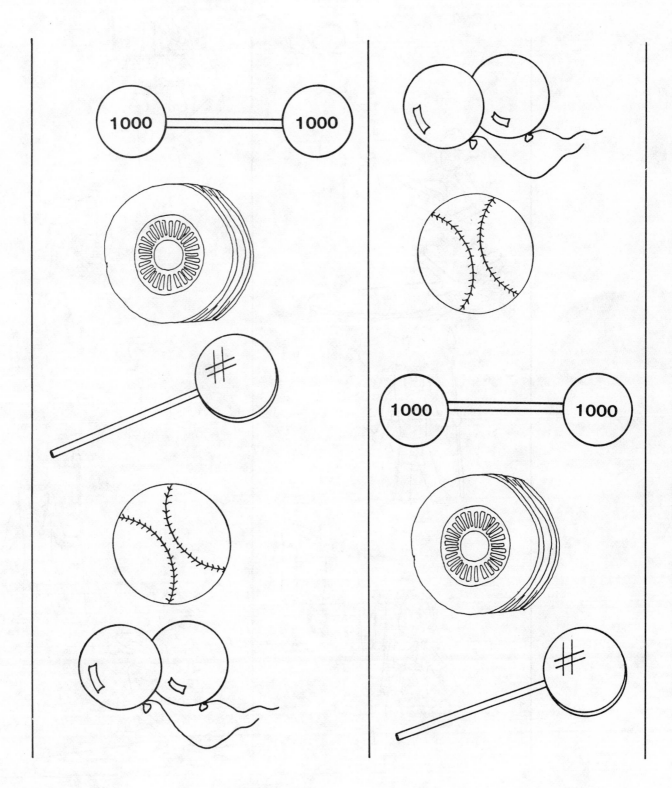

Purpose: To help the child see how things are alike and how they are different.

Directions: Ask the child to draw a line connecting the pictures that are exactly alike.

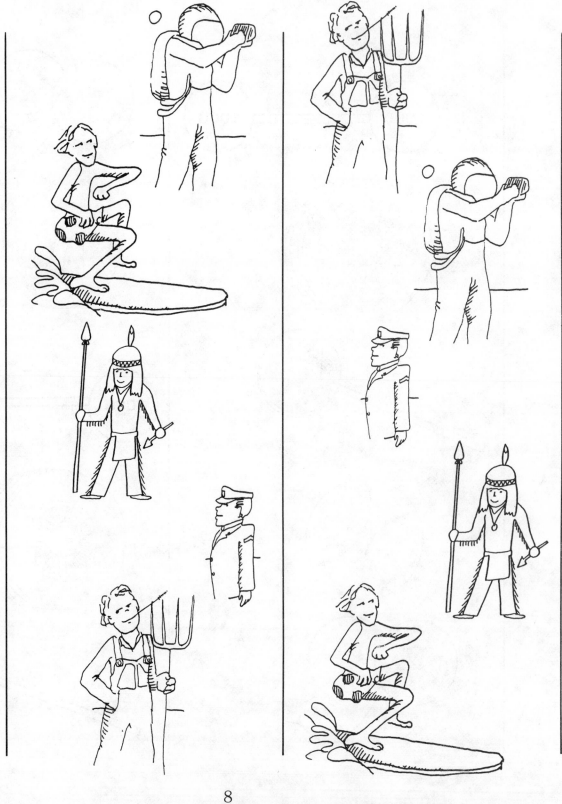

8

3

Purpose: To help the child learn to see details.

Directions: Ask the child to look at the pictures and tell you what is missing from each one. Ask the child to draw in the missing part.

Purpose: To help the child learn to see details.

Directions: Ask the child to look at the pictures and tell you what is missing from each one. Ask the child to draw in the missing parts.

Purpose: To help the child see how things are alike and how they are different.

Directions: Ask the child to look at the pictures and find the pickup truck, milk truck, family car, **tractor**, **race car**, sports car, motorcycle, and tractor trailer truck. Then ask the child to tell you how the vehicles are alike and how they are different. Have the child color the pictures.

Purpose: To help the child see how things are alike and how they are different.

Directions: Ask the child to look at the pictures and find the tug boat, row boat, shrimp boat, submarine, ocean liner, and motor boat. Then ask the child to tell you how the boats are alike and how they are different. Have the child color the pictures.

Purpose: To help the child see how things are alike and how they are different.

Directions: Ask the child to look at the pictures and find the monkey, horse, dog, bird, frog, **baby camel, mother camel, baby zebra, mother zebra.** Then ask the child to tell you how **the animals are alike** and how they are different. Have the child color the pictures.

Purpose: To help the child see how shapes and letters are alike and different.

Directions: Ask the child to trace the shapes and letters. Then ask the child to copy the shapes and letters.

14

Purpose: To help the child see how shapes are alike and different.

Directions: Ask the child to trace the shapes. Then ask the child to copy the shapes.

10

Purpose: To help the child learn to remember what he/she has seen.

Directions: Cut out the pictures. Place three pictures before the child and ask him to look at them. Then, while the child covers his eyes, shuffle the pictures and remove one. Ask the child to tell you which picture is missing. Repeat this activity several times.

11

Purpose: To help the child see how things are alike and how they are different.

Directions: Cut out the pictures. Shuffle the pictures and ask the child to match the pictures that are alike.

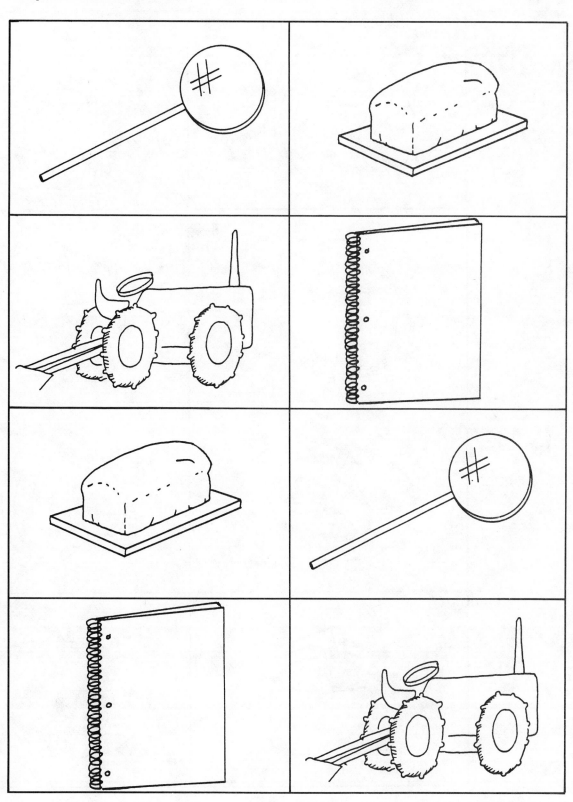

12

Purpose: To help the child see how things are alike and how they are different.

Directions: Cut out the pictures. Shuffle the pictures and ask the child to match the pictures that **are alike.**

13

Purpose: To help the child see how parts fit together to form a whole picture.

Directions: Cut the picture on the dotted lines into four pieces. Mix up the pieces and ask the child to put them back together the right way.

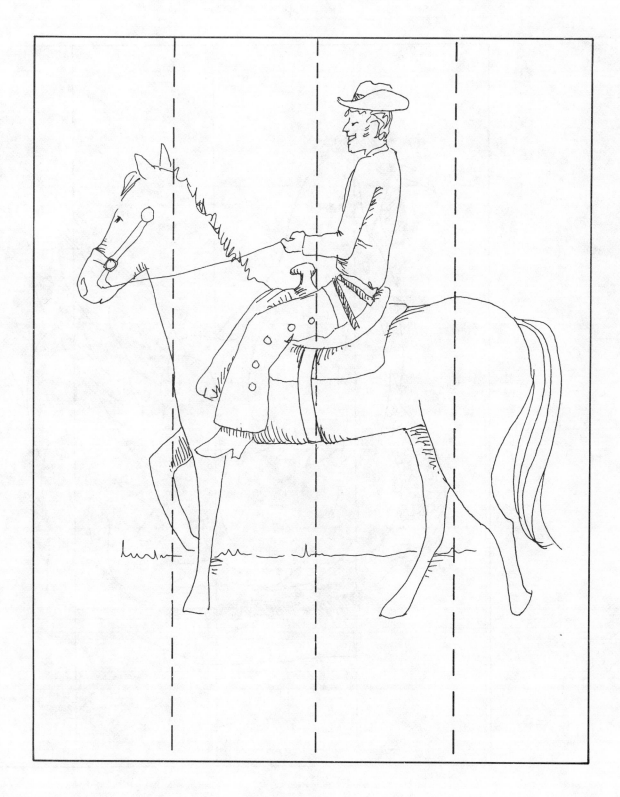

14

Purpose: To help the child see how parts fit together to form a whole picture.

Directions: Cut the picture on the dotted lines into four pieces. Mix up the pieces and ask the child to put them back together the right way.

15

Purpose: To help the child see how things are alike and how they are different.

Directions: Cut out the pictures. Ask the child to look at the three items in each picture and tell you which one is different from the other two, and why.

21

16

Purpose: To help the child see how things are alike and how they are different.

Directions: Cut out the pictures. Ask the child to look at the items in each picture and tell you how they are alike and how they are different.

17

Purpose: To help the child see how things are alike and how they are different.

Directions: Cut out the pictures. Ask the child to look at the four items in each picture and tell you how they are alike and how they are different.

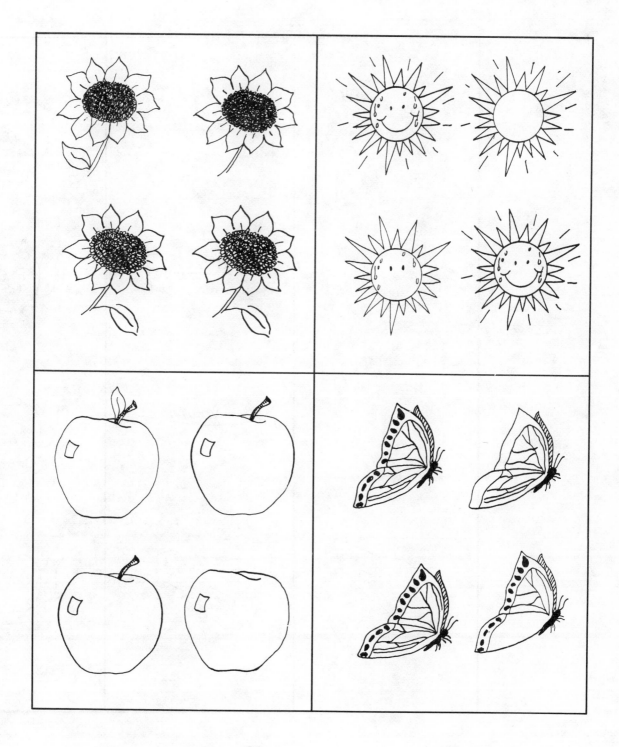

18

Purpose: To help the child see how things are alike and how they are different.

Directions: Cut out the pictures. Ask the child to look at the four items in each picture and tell you how they are alike and how they are different.

19

Purpose: To help the child see letters which are the same.

Directions: Ask the child to look at the three letters in each picture and tell you which two are alike. Tell the child the letter names.

A C A	F P F
R E E	B B R
X Y X	S Z S

Purpose: To help the child see letters which are the same.

Directions: Ask the child to look at the four letters in each picture and tell you which two are alike. Tell the child the letter names.

L L Y I	Q O D Q
F E T E	B D B P
M M N A	R P P B

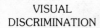

Purpose: To help the child see how words are alike and how they are different.

Directions: Ask the child to look at the word pairs and tell you whether they are the same or different. Ask the child to tell you how they are alike or different.

CAT CAT	RAT RAT
NOW NOT	AX AT
DOWN DOT	STAR STOP

Purpose: To help the child see how words are alike and how they are different.

Directions: Ask the child to look at the three words in each set and tell you which two are alike. Ask the child to tell you how the three words are alike or different.

OX HAS OX	WAS WAS TOO
ZOO ZOO SAW	THIS THE THE
GO GO TO	ARE ARE HERE

Auditory Discrimination

1

Purpose: To teach the child to hear rhyming words.

Directions: Read these jingles and have the child say them with you. Ask the child to tell you which words rhyme. You can color the pictures when you are finished.

Poor old Joe hit his toe with a hoe.

The goose got loose and chased the moose.

I want to bake a cake by the lake.

The socks and clock are on the rock.

We use a key to open the tree.

The king with a ring likes to sing.

Purpose: To teach the child to hear words that rhyme.

Directions: Read these jingles and have the child say them with you. Ask the child to tell you which words rhyme. You can color the pictures when you are finished.

They ran a race in outer space.

The dog chased the hog over a log.

Here is a dragon riding a wagon.

The man is taking a bath in a pan.

This is a nice old rook who loves to read a book:

We hopped in our car and drove very far.

Purpose: To teach the child to hear words that rhyme.

Directions: Read these jingles and have the child say them with you. Ask the child to tell you which words rhyme. You can color the pictures when you are finished.

Here is a goat in a sinking boat.

Here is a cat in a hat jumping on a rat.

This boat is floating in the castle's moat.

This bee is hiding behind a tree.

See the mouse run around the house.

Here is a fish living in a dish.

Purpose: To help the child learn to hear sounds that are alike and different.

Directions: Have the child make the sounds the objects in the pictures would make. Then you make the sound an object in one of the pictures would make and have the child point to the right picture.

5

Purpose: To help the child learn to hear sounds that are alike or different.

Directions: Have the child make the sounds the objects in the pictures would make. Then you make the sound an object in one of the pictures would make and have the child point to the right picture.

35

Purpose: To help the child practice remembering the sequence of phrases.

Directions: Read each line below and have the child repeat the phrases after you.

1. *See the cat.*
2. *See the cat in the tree.*
3. *See the cat in the tree who wants down.*

1. *Put on your hat.*
2. *Put on your hat to go outside.*
3. *Put on your hat to go outside and see Tommy.*

1. *Watch the goat.*
2. *Watch the goat climb a tree.*
3. *Watch the goat climb a tree to get an apple.*

1. *We got in the car.*
2. *We got in the car to go to the store.*
3. *We got in the car to go to the store to buy a kite.*

1. *Look up in the sky.*
2. *Look up in the sky and see the airplane.*
3. *Look up in the sky and see the airplane flying over the sun.*

Purpose: To help the child learn to listen.

Directions: Read the sequence of directions to the child and have him/her follow them in order. You may need to read the directions several times and very slowly to begin with.

Two Sequence Directions

1. Raise your hands and sing a song.
2. Touch your ear and pull your hair.
3. Go to the door and open/close it.
4. Stand up and walk around a chair.
5. Hop on one foot and say "Hello".

Three Sequence Directions

1. Go to the door, knock three times, and come back here.
2. Pull your nose, touch your ear, and tap your knee.
3. Sit on the floor, roll over, and stand up.
4. Touch your ear, say "Howdy Doody", and hop on one foot.
5. Raise your hands, pull your hair, and turn around.

Four Sequence Directions

1. Sit on the floor, roll over, stand up, and hop on one foot.
2. Sit down, stand up, sit down, and hide your eyes.
3. Wiggle your ears, touch your nose, hop on one foot, and touch a toe.
4. Go to the door, knock three times, come back, and sit down.
5. Crawl to the wall, stand up, walk backwards, and turn around.

Purpose: To help the child hear words that begin with the same sound.

Directions: Ask the child to listen while you read the word pairs and tell you if they have the same beginning sound or not.

boy	*balloon*
cat	*car*
house	*tall*
bat	*ball*
fog	*pain*
apple	*airplane*
jam	*car*
fog	*finger*
dog	*doll*
bat	*airplane*
log	*lamp*
leaf	*shoe*
goat	*gun*
dog	*plant*
jar	*jam*
pan	*pat*
cat	*doll*
tail	*tall*
mouse	*match*
balloon	*finger*
hat	*hammer*
pan	*can*

Purpose: To help the child hear words that begin with the same sound.

Directions: Ask the child to listen while you read the word pairs and tell you if they have the same beginning sound or not.

fan	*fall*
yellow	*pail*
rabbit	*race*
zoo	*lion*
water	*waste*
apple	*match*
zebra	*zoo*
ball	*dog*
vale	*varmint*
rat	*soap*
girl	*gale*

water	*goal*
kite	*kitchen*
value	*true*
sun	*sail*
log	*hammer*
yes	*yellow*
jam	*shoe*
cap	*call*
finger	*goose*
talk	*table*
fur	*kite*

10

Purpose: To help the child hear words that begin with the same sound.

Directions: Ask the child to name the items pictured in each pair and tell you if they begin with the same sound or a different sound.

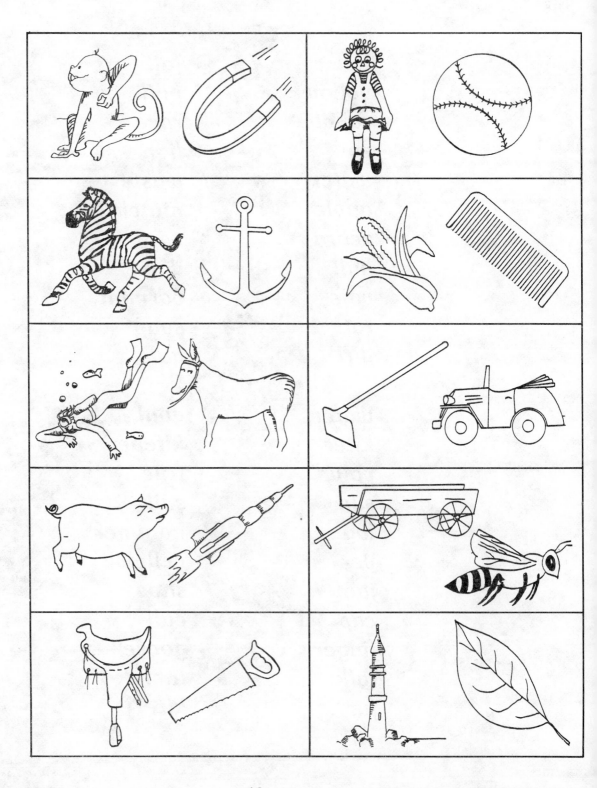

Purpose: To help the child hear words that begin with the same sound.

Directions: Ask the child to name the items pictured in each pair and tell you if they begin with the same sound or not.

12

Purpose: To help the child hear words that begin with the same sound.

Directions: Ask the child to name the items pictured in each pair and tell you if they begin with the same sound or not.

13

Purpose: To help the child hear words that begin with the same sound.

Directions: For each row of pictures, ask the child to name all the items pictured and to tell you which ones begin with the same sound as the first picture in that row.

Purpose: To help the child hear words that begin with the same sound.

Directions: For each row of pictures, ask the child to name all the items pictured and to tell you which ones begin with the same sound as the first picture in that row.

15

Purpose: To help the child hear words that begin with the same sound.

Directions: For each row of pictures, ask the child to name all the items pictured and tell you which ones begin with the same sound as the first picture in that row.

45

16

Purpose: To help the child hear words that begin with the same sound.

Directions: For each row of pictures, ask the child to name all the items pictured and tell you which ones begin with the same sound as the first picture in that row.

17

Purpose: To help the child hear rhyming sounds in words.

Directions: Ask the child to name the items in each picture pair and tell you if they rhyme or not.

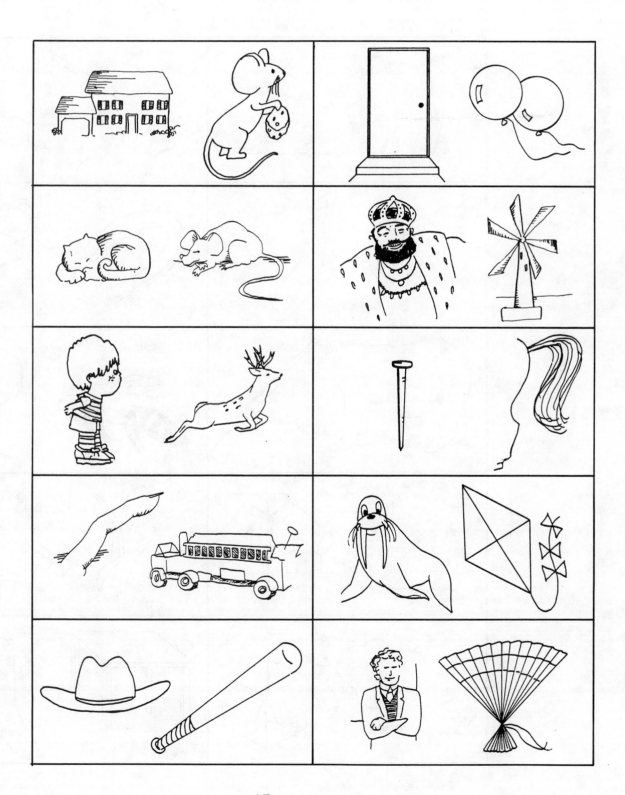

18

Purpose: To help the child hear rhyming sounds in words.

Directions: Ask the child to name items in each picture pair and tell you if they rhyme or not.

19

Purpose: To help the child learn to hear a sequence and remember what he/she has heard.

Directions: Ask the child to listen while you clap these patterns. Next ask the child to clap each pattern with you. Then clap a pattern and ask the child to repeat it by himself.

Purpose: To help the child learn to hear a sequence and remember what he/she has heard.

Directions: Read these groups of words and numbers to the child and ask him to repeat them to you. For further practice, read the words and numbers as written and have the child repeat them backwards.

2,2,1	5,3,5	7,4,6
1,7,3,	SUE HAT DOG	GO SOW LOT
LAP LAKE ON	NO TOE MOP	9,1,3,6
7,4,4,4	TO TO NO	FOR MAN THE

Learning
Letter Names

1

Purpose: To help the child learn the upper and lower case letter names.

Directions: Tell the child the name of the letter. Explain that both the upper and lower case letters have the same name. Then ask the child to name the pictures. Explain that each item pictured begins with the same letter. Have the child color the pictures. Next have the child practice writing the upper and lower case letters.

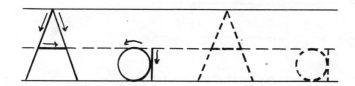

Purpose: To help the child learn the upper and lower case letter names.

Directions: Tell the child the name of the letter. Explain that both the upper and lower case letters have the same name. Then ask the child to name the pictures. Explain that each item pictured begins with the same letter. Have the child color the pictures. Next have the child practice writing the upper and lower case letters.

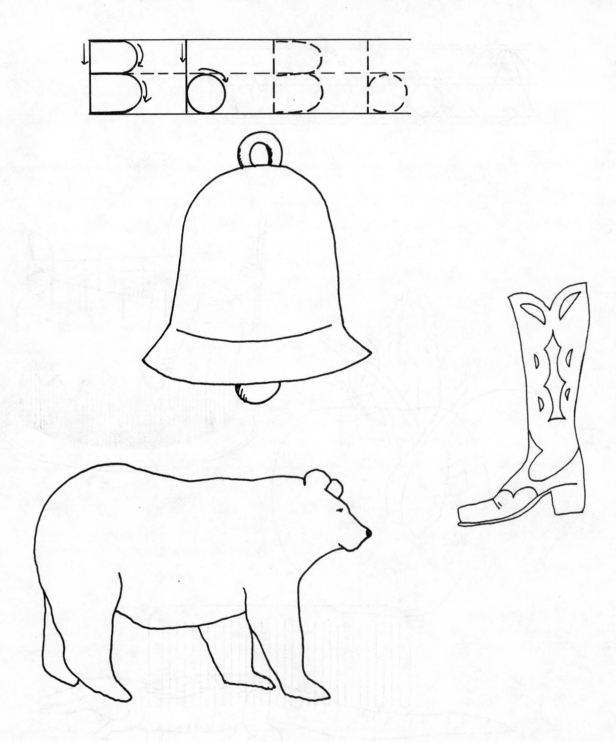

3

Purpose: To help the child learn the upper and lower case letter names.

Directions: Tell the child the name of the letter. Explain that both the upper and lower case letters have the same name. Then ask the child to name the pictures. Explain that each item pictured begins with the same letter. Have the child color the pictures. Next have the child practice writing the upper and lower case letters.

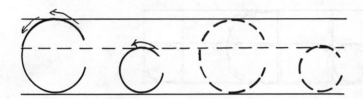

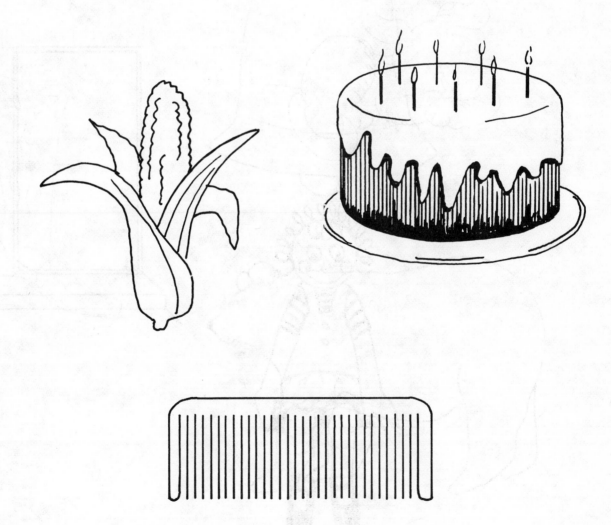

Purpose: To help the child learn the upper and lower case letter names.

Directions: Tell the child the name of the letter. Explain that both the upper and lower case letters have the same name. Then ask the child to name the pictures. Explain that each item pictured begins with the same letter. Have the child color the pictures. Next have the child practice writing the upper and lower case letters.

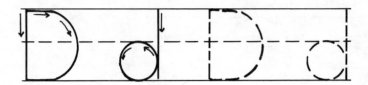

Purpose: To help the child learn the upper and lower case letter names.

Directions: Tell the child the name of the letter. Explain that both the upper and lower case letters have the same name. Then ask the child to name the pictures. Explain that each item pictured begins with the same letter. Have the child color the pictures. Next have the child practice writing the upper and lower case letters.

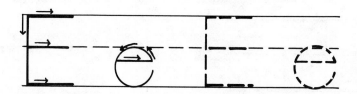

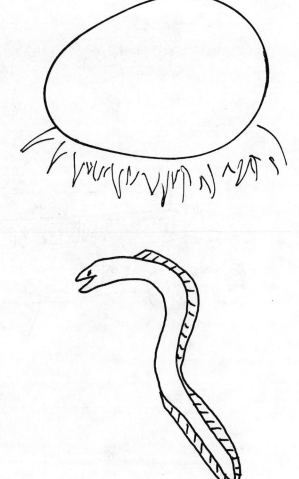

Purpose: To help the child learn the upper and lower case letter names.

Directions: Tell the child the name of the letter. Explain that both the upper and lower case letters have the same name. Then ask the child to name the pictures. Explain that each item pictured begins with the same letter. Have the child color the pictures. Next have the child practice writing the upper and lower case letters.

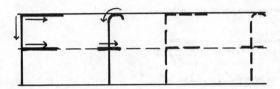

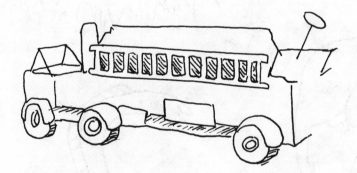

Purpose: To help the child learn the upper and lower case letter names.

Directions: Tell the child the name of the letter. Explain that both the upper and lower case letters have the same name. Then ask the child to name the pictures. Explain that each item pictured begins with the same letter. Have the child color the pictures. Next have the child practice writing the upper and lower case letters.

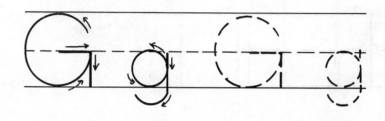

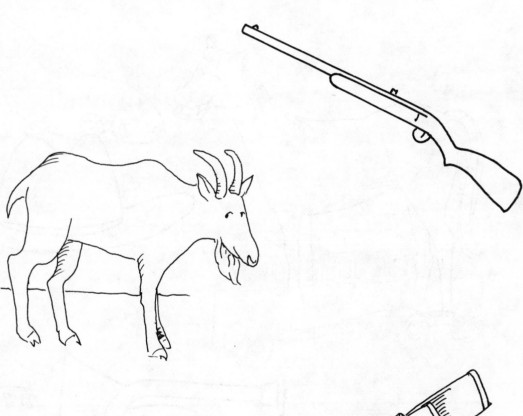

Purpose: To help the child learn the upper and lower case letter names.

Directions: Tell the child the name of the letter. Explain that both the upper and lower case letters have the same name. Then ask the child to name the pictures. Explain that each item pictured begins with the same letter. Have the child color the pictures. Next have the child practice writing the upper and lower case letters.

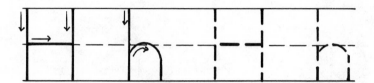

60

Purpose: To help the child learn the upper and lower case letter names.

Directions: Tell the child the name of the letter. Explain that both the upper and lower case letters have the same name. Then ask the child to name the pictures. Explain that each item pictured begins with the same letter. Have the child color the pictures. Next have the child practice writing the upper and lower case letters.

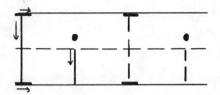

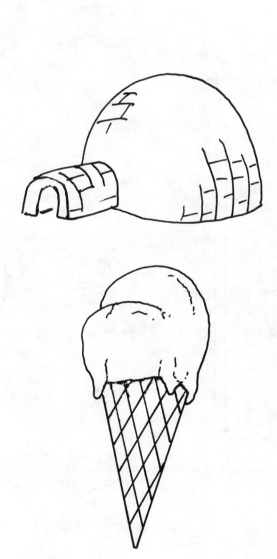

10

Purpose: To help the child learn the upper and lower case letter names.

Directions: Tell the child the name of the letter. Explain that both the upper and lower case letters have the same name. Then ask the child to name the pictures. Explain that each item pictured begins with the same letter. Have the child color the pictures. Next have the child practice writing the upper and lower case letters.

11

Purpose: To help the child learn the upper and lower case letter names.

Directions: Tell the child the name of the letter. Explain that both the upper and lower case letters have the same name. Then ask the child to name the pictures. Explain that each item pictured begins with the same letter. Have the child color the pictures. Next have the child practice writing the upper and lower case letters.

12

Purpose: To help the child learn the upper and lower case letter names.

Directions: Tell the child the name of the letter. Explain that both the upper and lower case letters have the same name. Then ask the child to name the pictures. Explain that each item pictured begins with the same letter. Have the child color the pictures. Next have the child practice writing the upper and lower case letters.

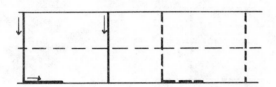

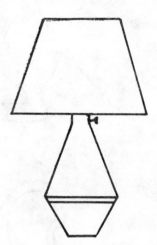

13

Purpose: To help the child learn the upper and lower case letter names.

Directions: Tell the child the name of the letter. Explain that both the upper and lower case letters have the same name. Then ask the child to name the pictures. Explain that each item pictured begins with the same letter. Have the child color the pictures. Next have the child practice writing the upper and lower case letters.

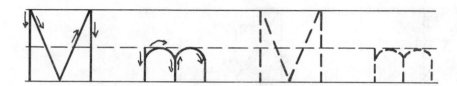

MILK

14

Purpose: To help the child learn the upper and lower case letter names.

Directions: Tell the child the name of the letter. Explain that both the upper and lower case letters have the same name. Then ask the child to name the pictures. Explain that each item pictured begins with the same letter. Have the child color the pictures. Next have the child practice writing the upper and lower case letters.

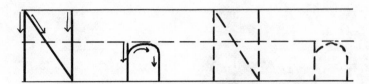

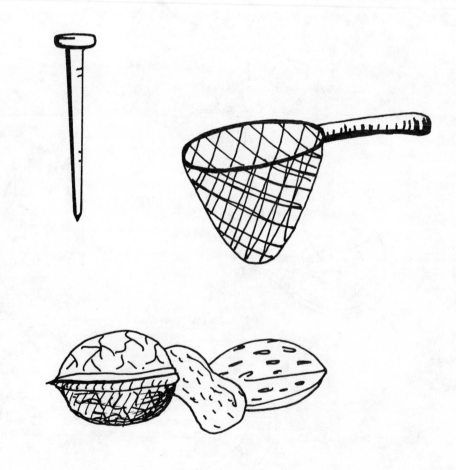

15

Purpose: To help the child learn the upper and lower case letter names.

Directions: Tell the child the name of the letter. Explain that both the upper and lower case letters have the same name. Then ask the child to name the pictures. Explain that each item pictured begins with the same letter. Have the child color the pictures. Next have the child practice writing the upper and lower case letters.

67

16

Purpose: To help the child learn the upper and lower case letter names.

Directions: Tell the child the name of the letter. Explain that both the upper and lower case letters have the same name. Then ask the child to name the pictures. Explain that each item pictured begins with the same letter. Have the child color the pictures. Next have the child practice writing the upper and lower case letters.

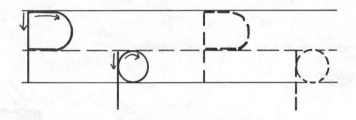

17

Purpose: To help the child learn the upper and lower case letter names.

Directions: Tell the child the name of the letter. Explain that both the upper and lower case letters have the same name. Then ask the child to name the pictures. Explain that each item pictured begins with the same letter. Have the child color the pictures. Next have the child practice writing the upper and lower case letters.

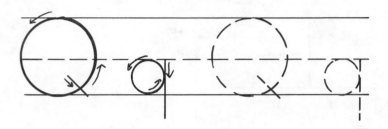

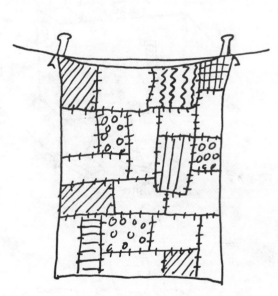

69

18

Purpose: To help the child learn the upper and lower case letter names.

Directions: Tell the child the name of the letter. Explain that both the upper and lower case letters have the same name. Then ask the child to name the pictures. Explain that each item pictured begins with the same letter. Have the child color the pictures. Next have the child practice writing the upper and lower case letters.

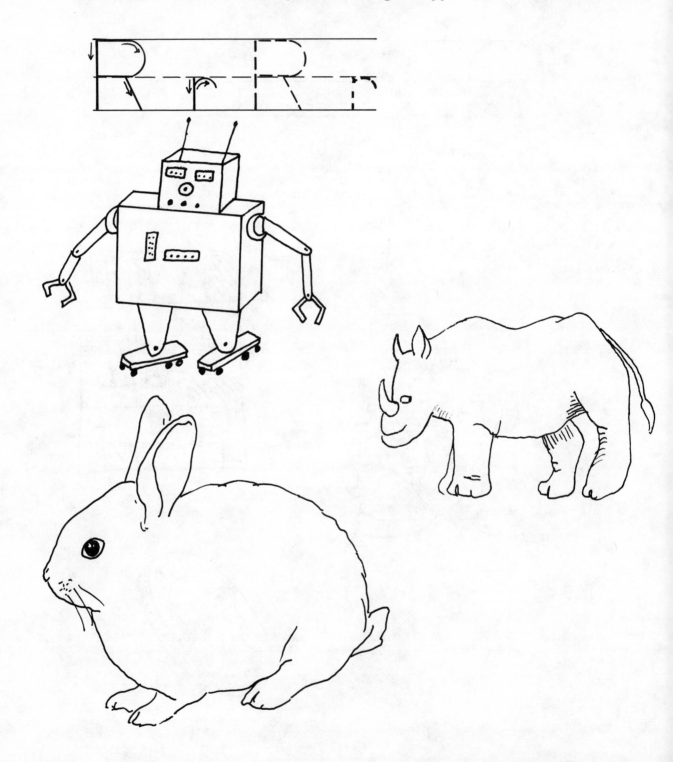

19

Purpose: To help the child learn the upper and lower case letter names.

Directions: Tell the child the name of the letter. Explain that both the upper and lower case letters have the same name. Then ask the child to name the pictures. Explain that each item pictured begins with the same letter. Have the child color the pictures. Next have the child practice writing the upper and lower case letters.

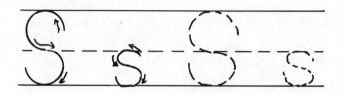

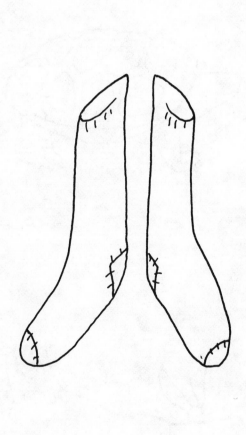

Purpose: To help the child learn the upper and lower case letter names.

Directions: Tell the child the name of the letter. Explain that both the upper and lower case letters have the same name. Then ask the child to name the pictures. Explain that each item pictured begins with the same letter. Have the child color the pictures. Next have the child practice writing the upper and lower case letters.

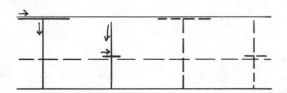

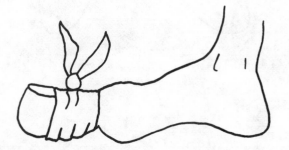

72

21

Purpose: To help the child learn the upper and lower case letter names.

Directions: Tell the child the name of the letter. Explain that both the upper and lower case letters have the same name. Then ask the child to name the pictures. Explain that each item pictured begins with the same letter. Have the child color the pictures. Next have the child practice writing the upper and lower case letters.

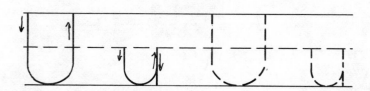

22 Purpose: To help the child learn the upper and lower case letter names.

Directions: Tell the child the name of the letter. Explain that both the upper and lower case letters have the same name. Then ask the child to name the pictures. Explain that each item pictured begins with the same letter. Have the child color the pictures. Next have the child practice writing the upper and lower case letters.

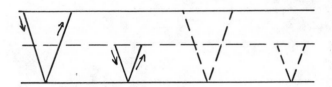

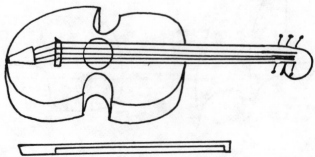

23

Purpose: To help the child learn the upper and lower case letter names.

Directions: Tell the child the name of the letter. Explain that both the upper and lower case letters have the same name. Then ask the child to name the pictures. Explain that each item pictured begins with the same letter. Have the child color the pictures. Next have the child practice writing the upper and lower case letters.

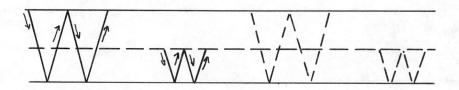

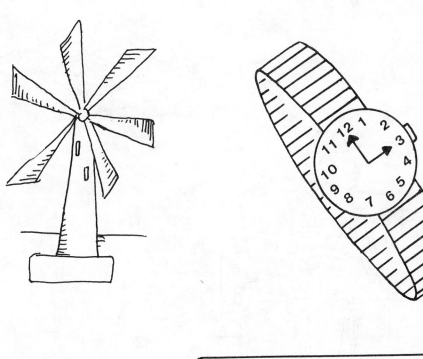

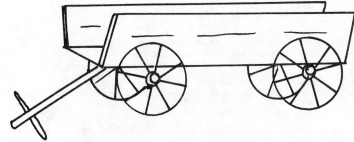

24

Purpose: To help the child learn the upper and lower case letter names.

Directions: Tell the child the name of the letter. Explain that both the upper and lower case letters have the same name. Then ask the child to name the pictures. Explain that each item pictured begins with the same letter. Have the child color the pictures. Next have the child practice writing the upper and lower case letters.

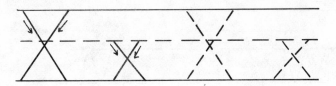

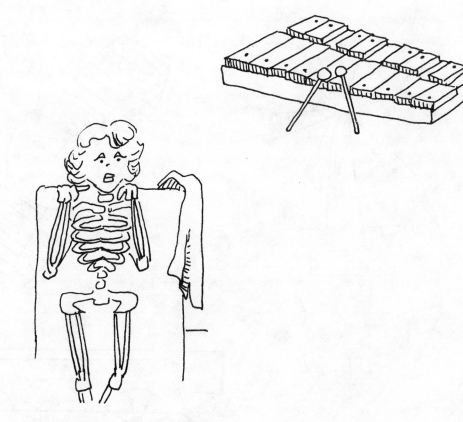

25 Purpose: To help the child learn the upper and lower case letter names.

Directions: Tell the child the name of the letter. Explain that both the upper and lower case letters have the same name. Then ask the child to name the pictures. Explain that each item pictured begins with the same letter. Have the child color the pictures. Next have the child practice writing the upper and lower case letters.

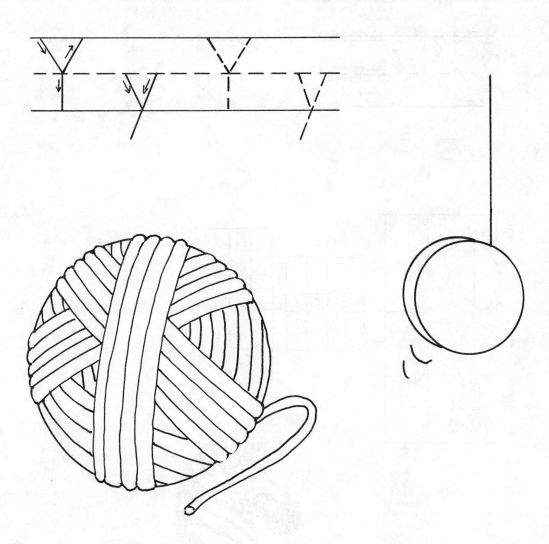

26

Purpose: To help the child learn the upper and lower case letter names.

Directions: Tell the child the name of the letter. Explain that both the upper and lower case letters have the same name. Then ask the child to name the pictures. Explain that each item pictured begins with the same letter. Have the child color the pictures. Next have the child practice writing the upper and lower case letters.

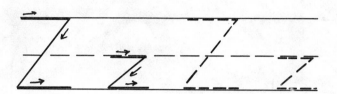

27 **Purpose:** To help the child learn the upper case letter names.

Directions: Name a letter and ask the child to point to it. Repeat. Then, point to a letter and ask the child to name it. Repeat.

A	B	C	D
E	F	G	H
I	J	K	L
M	N	O	P
Q	R	S	T
U	V	W	X
Y	Z	B	M

 **Purpose:** To help the child learn the lower case letter names.

Directions: Name a letter and ask the child to point to it. Repeat. Then, point to a letter and ask the child to name it. Repeat.

a	b	c	d
e	f	g	h
i	j	k	l
m	n	o	p
q	r	s	t
u	v	w	x
y	z	b	d

Purpose: To help the child learn the letter names.

Directions: Cut out the letters. Turn them face down and play Concentration. Take turns turning the pictures right side up, two at a time, trying to match pairs. If the pair matches, set them aside. If the pair doesn't match, turn them face down again.

B	B	D	D
C	C	G	G
M	M	W	W
E	E	F	F
L	L	T	T
N	N	P	P

81

30 Purpose: To help the child learn the names of upper and lower case letters.

Directions: Cut out the letters. Turn them face down and play Concentration. Take turns turning the pictures right side up, two at a time, trying to match the pairs of upper and lower case letters. If the pair matches, set them aside. If the pair doesn't match, turn them face down again.

A	a	B	b
D	d	E	e
M	m	N	n
P	p	Q	q
R	r	l	i
G	g	H	h

Phonics

To the Parent:

Phonics is concerned with speech sounds and the letters, letter groups, and syllables which represent those sounds in reading and spelling. Sometimes a single letter may represent a speech sound, as is the case with letter *f* in *fan*. At other times several letters may be required to represent a speech sound, as is the case with **ing** in the word **sing: s-ing**.

Phonics is based upon the principle that when words are spelled alike, they probably sound alike. Words that are "phonetic" are words which are spelled as they sound and sound as they are spelled. In our language not all words are **phonetically regular.** That is, not all words are spelled exactly as they sound. But even with irregular words, phonics can often help with the beginning or ending sounds, or the vowel sounds. It is said that in the English language there are only two words-**who** and **eye**-with which phonics would be of no help.

Studies show that about 86% of all of the **syllables** in our language are spelled as they sound. That means that about 14% of the syllables do not sound the way you would expect them to from the way they are spelled. But the child who knows phonics should be able to read and write most of the syllables in the words he will use. You see why phonics is so important.

A good reader knows by sight almost every word he comes to in his reading. If he comes to a word he does not know by sight, the reader must stop and pay attention to that unknown word. Sometimes the meaning of the unknown word is suggested by the context in which it is used, or the meaning of the other words in the sentence. At times, a reader recognizes a part of the unknown word which, combined with its context, quickly suggests to him what the word is. It isn't always necessary to sound out each letter and syllable of the entire word and blend the sounds together to recognize the word.

For example, if the young reader sees the sentence, "He wanted a new car so he bought an Oldsmobile," he might not recognize the word **Oldsmobile**. If the reader is rather familiar with cars he might get the word by looking at the first letter: **O--------.** If the first letter is not adequate, the reader may need to see the syllable **Olds------,** which for many would be a clue to the entire word. If no other clue worked, the reader might need to sound out, letter by letter, **O-l-d-s-(Olds) m-o-(mo) b-i-l-e(bile)** and blend the sounds together to form the word **Oldsmobile.** (From his knowledge of cars he will probably know the last syllable does not rhyme with "mile.")

Now, this is phonics at work. A good reader has a large sight vocabulary so that he recognizes many words instantly. In order to pronounce a word which he does not recognize on sight, the reader must sometimes use his knowledge of letter combinations and the sounds they represent. He uses phonics along with context and structural analysis (knowledge of prefixes, suffixes, syllables, etc.) to identify an unknown word. A good reader has a good balance of these skills and knows how to use them together.

Phonics skills are necessary. You can not be a good reader (or a good speller) if you do not know, and cannot use in a functional way, the relationship between letters and sounds. Many alert readers recognize for themselves the relationship between letters and letter combinations and sounds. Through many contacts with words, the young reader may discover that, generally, words which begin with the same letters begin with the same sounds and those which end with the same letters end with the same sounds. He may discover other important things about phonics in the same way. **But phonics is too important to be left to chance.** Since you cannot be a good reader without phonics skills, teachers teach children all about letters and the sounds which they represent. Throughout the early grades, reading books are planned to teach the phonics skills in an orderly, sequential way.

Some children learn phonics quickly and easily. Others find it quite difficult and need a lot of individual help and practice. Often the teacher can not find the time to give a child all the individual help he needs. The willing parent can do much to help his child learn phonics by carrying out the activities suggested by the teacher.

1

Purpose: To help your child learn the sound associated with the letter **B** at the beginning of a word.

Directions: 1.   Have your child say the name of each item pictured. Point out that they all begin with the same sound. Have your child say other words which begin the same way. Pronounce some words which begin with **B** and some which do not and have your child tell you which is which.

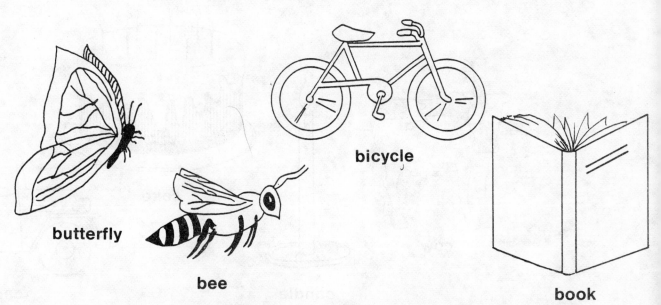

butterfly

bee

bicycle

book

2.   Have your child look at the name of each item pictured and say it aloud. Point out that the name of each picture begins with the letter **B** and they all begin with the same sound. Be sure your child understands the sound associated with the letter **B** at the beginning of a word.

3.   Be certain that your child knows the letter **B** and can write it. Number several lines on a piece of paper. Pronounce several words which begin with the letter **B** and some which do not. Have your child write the letter **B** in the proper space for each word which begins with **B**. He may leave the other spaces blank.

4.   In magazines or catalogues, let your child find pictures whose names begin with the letter **B**. He may cut out these pictures and place them in an envelope marked **B** and use them for further practice. Have fun with your child by making up sentences which have several words beginning with the letter **B**. (The boy bought a bag of books.)

Purpose: To help your child learn the sound associated with the letter **C** (hard sound) at the beginning of a word.

Directions: 1. Have your child say the name of each item pictured. Point out that they all begin with the same sound. Have your child say other words which begin the same way. Pronounce some words which begin with **C** and some which do not and have your child tell you which is which.

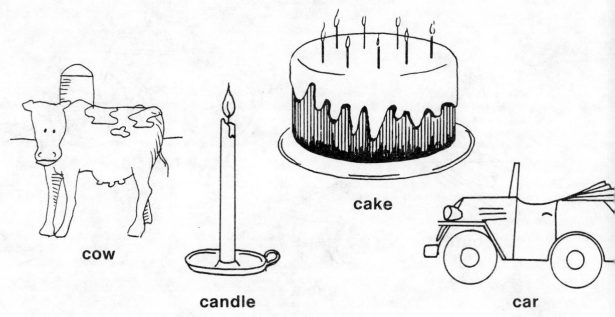

cow

candle

cake

car

2. Have your child look at the name of each item pictured and say it aloud. Point out that the name of each picture begins with the letter **C** and they all begin with the same sound. Be sure your child understands the sound associated with the letter **C** at the beginning of a word.

3. Be certain that your child knows the letter **C** and can write it. Number several lines on a piece of paper. Pronounce several words which begin with the letter **C** and some which do not. Have your child write the letter **C** in the proper space for each word which begins with **C**. He may leave the other spaces blank.

4. In magazines or catalogues, let your child find pictures whose names begin with the letter "hard **C**." He may cut out these pictures and place them in an envelope marked **C** and use them for further practice. Have fun with your child by making up sentences which have several words beginning with the letter **C**. (The cat can cut the cake.)

Purpose: To help your child learn the **S** sound of **C** at the beginning of words.

Directions: 1.   Have your child say the name of each item pictured. Point out that they all begin with the same sound. It is the **S** sound represented by the letter **C**. (In some words **C** represents the sound of **K**, as in *cat*.)

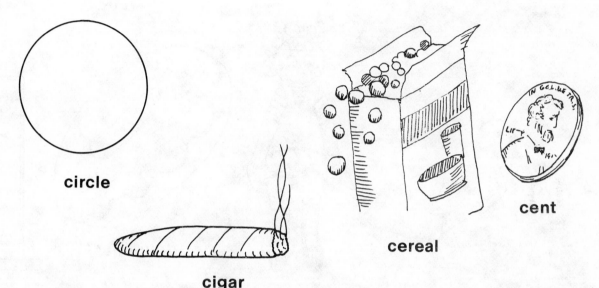

circle

cent

cereal

cigar

2.   Have your child look at the name of each item pictured and say it aloud. Point out that the name of each picture begins with the letter **C** and that in some words **C** represents the sound of **S**. Help your child understand the sound associated with the letter **C** at the beginning of these words.

3.   Be certain that your child knows the letter **C** and can write it. Number several lines on a piece of paper. Pronounce several words which begin with the letter **C** and sound like **S** and some which do not. Have your child write the letter **C** in the proper space for each word in which **C** sounds like **S**. Leave the other spaces blank.

4.   In magazines or catalogues, let your child find pictures whose names begin with **C** and sound like **S**. He may cut out these pictures and place them in an envelope marked "soft **C**" and use them for further practice. Have fun with your child by making up sentences which have several words beginning with **C** representing the sound of **S**. (You can go to the circus in the city for a cent.)

89

Purpose: To help your child learn the sound associated with the letter *D* at the beginning of a word.

Directions: 1. Have your child say the name of each item pictured. Point out that they all begin with the same sound. Have your child say other words which begin the same way. Pronounce some words which begin with *D* and some which do not and have your child tell you which is which.

duck   **doll**   **doughnut**   **door**

2. Have your child look at the name of each item pictured and say it aloud. Point out that the name of each picture begins with the letter *D* and they all begin with the same sound. Be sure your child understands the sound associated with the letter *D* at the beginning of a word.

3. Be certain that your child knows the letter *D* and can write it. Number several lines on a piece of paper. Pronounce several words which begin with the letter *D* and some which do not. Have your child write the letter *D* in the proper space for each word which begins with *D*. He may leave the other spaces blank.

4. In magazines or catalogues, let your child find pictures whose names begin with the letter *D*. He may cut out these pictures and place them in an envelope marked *D* and use them for further practice. Have fun with your child by making up sentences which have several words beginning with the letter *D*. (The dog ran the duck and the deer through the door.)

Purpose: To help your child learn the sound associated with the letter **F** at the beginning of a word.

Directions: 1. Have your child say the name of each item pictured. Point out that they all begin with the same sound. Have your child say other words which begin the same way. Pronounce some words which begin with **F** and some which do not and have your child tell you which is which.

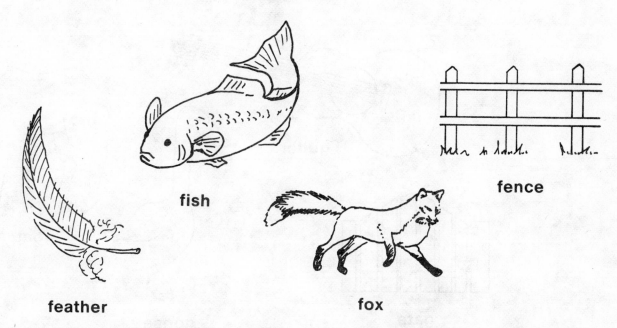

feather **fish** **fox** **fence**

2. Have your child look at the name of each item pictured and say it aloud. Point out that the name of each picture begins with the letter **F** and they all begin with the same sound. Be sure your child understands the sound associated with the letter **F** at the beginning of a word.

3. Be certain that your child knows the letter **F** and can write it. Number several lines on a piece of paper. Pronounce several words which begin with the letter **F** and some which do not. Have your child write the letter **F** in the proper space for each word which begins with **F**. He may leave the other spaces blank.

4. In magazines or catalogues, let your child find pictures whose names begin with the letter **F**. He may cut out these pictures and place them in an envelope marked **F** and use them for further practice. Have fun with your child by making up sentences which have several words beginning with the letter **F**. (The funny fox had feathers on his foot.)

Purpose: To help your child learn the hard sound associated with the letter **G** at the beginning of a word.

Directions: 1. Have your child say the name of each item pictured. Point out that they all begin with the same sound. Have your child say other words which begin the same way. Pronounce some words which begin with a hard **G** and some which do not and have your child tell you which is which.

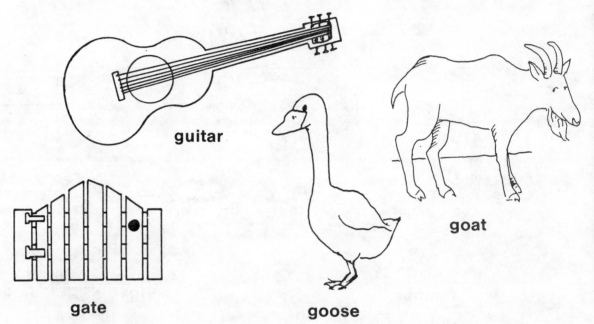

guitar

gate

goose

goat

2. Have your child look at the name of each item pictured and say it aloud. Point out that the name of each picture begins with the letter **G** and they all begin with the same sound. Be sure your child understands the hard sound associated with the letter **G** at the beginning of a word.

3. Be certain that your child knows the letter **G** and can write it. Number several lines on a piece of paper. Pronounce several words which begin with the hard letter **G** and some which do not. Have your child write the letter **G** in the proper space for each word which begins with a hard **G**. He may leave the other spaces blank.

4. In magazines or catalogues, let your child find pictures whose names begin with the hard letter **G**. He may cut out these pictures and place them in an envelope marked "Hard **G**" and use them for further practice. Have fun with your child by making up sentences which have several words beginning with the hard letter **G**. (The ghost frightened the goose and the goat through the gate.)

Purpose: To help your child learn the soft sound associated with the letter **G** at the beginning of a word.

Directions: 1.   Have your child say the name of each item pictured. Point out that they all begin with the same sound. Have your child say other words which begin the same way. Pronounce some words which begin with a soft **G** (or **J**) sound and some which do not and have your child tell you which is which.

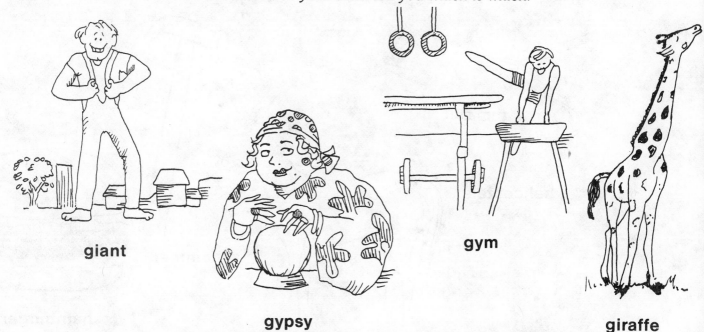

giant

gypsy

gym

giraffe

2.   Have your child look at the name of each item pictured and say it aloud. Point out that the name of each picture begins with the letter **G** and they all begin with the same sound. Be sure your child understands the soft sound associated with the letter **G** at the beginning of a word.

3.   Be certain that your child knows the letter **G** and can write it. Number several lines on a piece of paper. Pronounce several words which begin with the soft letter **G** and some which do not. Have your child write the letter **G** in the proper space for each word which begins with a soft **G**. He may leave the other spaces blank.

4.   In magazines or catalogues, let your child find pictures whose names begin with the soft letter **G**. He may cut out these pictures and place them in an envelope marked "Soft **G**" and use them for further practice. Have fun with your child by making up sentences which have several words beginning with the soft letter **G**. (The giant giraffe ran into the gym and caught germs.)

Purpose: To help your child learn the sound associated with the letter **H** at the beginning of a word.

Directions: 1.   Have your child say the name of each item pictured. Point out that they all begin with the same sound. Have your child say other words which begin the same way. Pronounce some words which begin with **H** and some which do not and have your child tell you which is which.

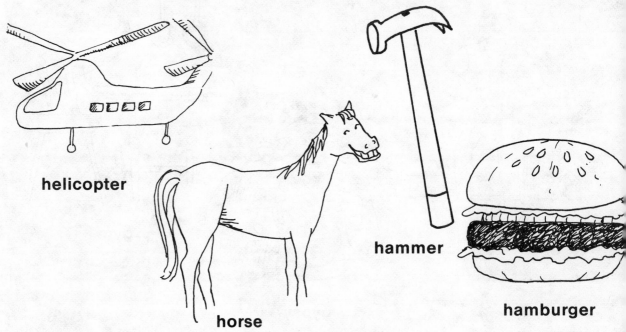

helicopter

horse

hammer

hamburger

2.   Have your child look at the name of each item pictured and say it aloud. Point out that the name of each picture begins with the letter **H** and they all begin with the same sound. Be sure your child understands the sound associated with the letter **H** at the beginning of a word.

3.   Be certain that your child knows the letter **H** and can write it. Number several lines on a piece of paper. Pronounce several words which begin with the letter **H** and some which do not. Have your child write the letter **H** in the proper space for each word which begins with **H**. He may leave the other spaces blank.

4.   In magazines or catalogues, let your child find pictures whose names begin with the letter **H**. He may cut out these pictures and place them in an envelope marked **H** and use them for further practice. Have fun with your child by making up sentences which have several words beginning with the letter **H**. (Henry hid the horse in the house.)

Purpose: To help your child learn the sound associated with the letter **J** at the beginning of a word.

Directions: 1. Have your child say the name of each item pictured. Point out that they all begin with the same sound. Have your child say other words which begin the same way. Pronounce some words which begin with **J** and some which do not and have your child tell you which is which.

jar

jug

jack-o-lantern

jack-in-the-box

2. Have your child look at the name of each item pictured and say it aloud. Point out that the name of each picture begins with the letter **J** and they all begin with the same sound. Be sure your child understands the sound associated with the letter **J** at the beginning of a word.

3. Be certain that your child knows the letter **J** and can write it. Number several lines on a piece of paper. Pronounce several words which begin with the letter **J** and some which do not. Have your child write the letter **J** in the proper space for each word which begins with **J**. He may leave the other spaces blank.

4. In magazines or catalogues, let your child find pictures whose names begin with the letter **J**. He may cut out these pictures and place them in an envelope marked **J** and use them for further practice. Have fun with your child by making up sentences which have several words beginning with the letter **J**. (Jump over the jack-o-lantern and into the jeep.)

10

Purpose: To help your child learn the sound associated with the letter **K** at the beginning of a word.

Directions: 1. Have your child say the name of each item pictured. Point out that they all begin with the same sound. Have your child say other words which begin the same way. Pronounce some words which begin with **K** and some which do not and have your child tell you which is which.

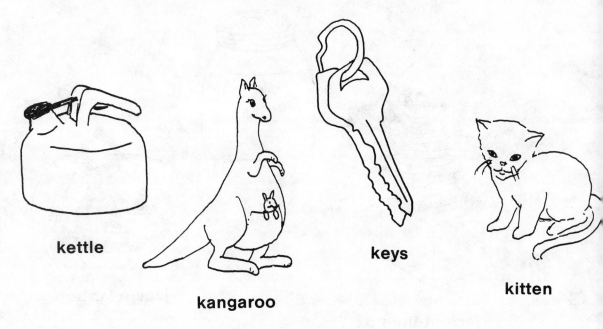

kettle

kangaroo

keys

kitten

2. Have your child look at the name of each item pictured and say it aloud. Point out that the name of each picture begins with the letter **K** and they all begin with the same sound. Be sure your child understands the sound associated with the letter **K** at the beginning of a word.

3. Be certain that your child knows the letter **K** and can write it. Number several lines on a piece of paper. Pronounce several words which begin with the letter **K** and some which do not. Have your child write the letter **K** in the proper space for each word which begins with **K**. He may leave the other spaces blank.

4. In magazines or catalogues, let your child find pictures whose names begin with the letter **K**. He may cut out these pictures and place them in an envelope marked **K** and use them for further practice. Have fun with your child by making up sentences which have several words beginning with the letter **K**. (The king had some keys, kittens, and a kite.)

11

Purpose: To help your child learn the sound associated with the letter **L** at the beginning of a word.

Directions: 1. Have your child say the name of each item pictured. Point out that they all begin with the same sound. Have your child say other words which begin the same way. Pronounce some words which begin with **L** and some which do not and have your child tell you which is which.

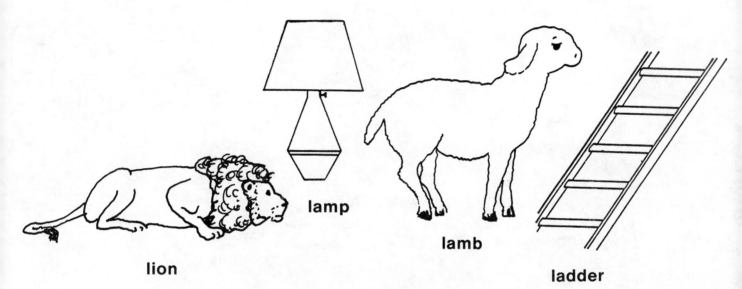

lamp

lamb

lion

ladder

2. Have your child look at the name of each item pictured and say it aloud. Point out that the name of each picture begins with the letter **L** and they all begin with the same sound. Be sure your child understands the sound associated with the letter **L** at the beginning of a word.

3. Be certain that your child knows the letter **L** and can write it. Number several lines on a piece of paper. Pronounce several words which begin with the letter **L** and some which do not. Have your child write the letter **L** in the proper space for each word which begins with **L**. He may leave the other spaces blank.

4. In magazines or catalogues, let your child find pictures whose names begin with the letter **L**. He may cut out these pictures and place them in an envelope marked **L** and use them for further practice. Have fun with your child by making up sentences which have several words beginning with the letter **L**. (Let the lion and the lamb climb the ladder.)

12

Purpose: To help your child learn the sound associated with the letter ***M*** at the beginning of a word.

Directions: 1. Have your child say the name of each item pictured. Point out that they all begin with the same sound. Have your child say other words which begin the same way. Pronounce some words which begin with ***M*** and some which do not and have your child tell you which is which.

mask

mouse

monkey

milk

2. Have your child look at the name of each item pictured and say it aloud. Point out that the name of each picture begins with the letter ***M*** and they all begin with the same sound. Be sure your child understands the sound associated with the letter ***M*** at the beginning of a word.

3. Be certain that your child knows the letter ***M*** and can write it. Number several lines on a piece of paper. Pronounce several words which begin with the letter ***M*** and some which do not. Have your child write the letter ***M*** in the proper space for each word which begins with ***M***. He may leave the other spaces blank.

4. In magazines or catalogues, let your child find pictures whose names begin with the letter ***M***. He may cut out these pictures and place them in an envelope marked ***M*** and use them for further practice. Have fun with your child by making up sentences which have several words beginning with the letter ***M***. (The monkey and the mouse played marbles with a mule.)

13

Purpose: To help your child learn the sound associated with the letter **N** at the beginning of a word.

Directions: 1.   Have your child say the name of each item pictured. Point out that they all begin with the same sound. Have your child say other words which begin the same way. Pronounce some words which begin with **N** and some which do not and have your child tell you which is which.

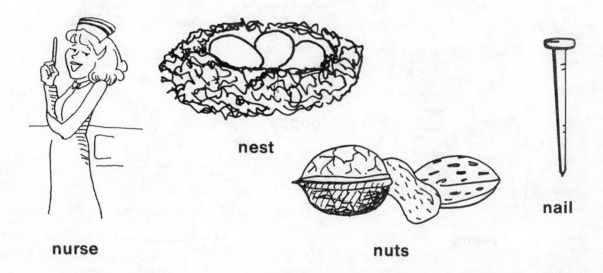

nurse   **nest**   **nuts**   **nail**

2.   Have your child look at the name of each item pictured and say it aloud. Point out that the name of each picture begins with the letter **N** and they all begin with the same sound. Be sure your child understands the sound associated with the letter **N** at the beginning of a word.

3.   Be certain that your child knows the letter **N** and can write it. Number several lines on a piece of paper. Pronounce several words which begin with the letter **N** and some which do not. Have your child write the letter **N** in the proper space for each word which begins with **N**. He may leave the other spaces blank.

4.   In magazines or catalogues, let your child find pictures whose names begin with the letter **N**. He may cut out these pictures and place them in an envelope marked **N** and use them for further practice. Have fun with your child by making up sentences which have several words beginning with the letter **N**. (Now the nurse comes with the needle.)

14

Purpose: To help your child learn the sound associated with the letter **P** at the beginning of a word.

Directions: 1.   Have your child say the name of each item pictured. Point out that they all begin with the same sound. Have your child say other words which begin the same way. Pronounce some words which begin with **P** and some which do not and have your child tell you which is which.

puppy

piano

pencil

pie

2.   Have your child look at the name of each item pictured and say it aloud. Point out that the name of each picture begins with the letter **P** and they all begin with the same sound. Be sure your child understands the sound associated with the letter **P** at the beginning of a word.

3.   Be certain that your child knows the letter **P** and can write it. Number several lines on a piece of paper. Pronounce several words which begin with the letter **P** and some which do not. Have your child write the letter **P** in the proper space for each word which begins with **P**. He may leave the other spaces blank.

4.   In magazines or catalogues, let your child find pictures whose names begin with the letter **P**. He may cut out these pictures and place them in an envelope marked **P** and use them for further practice. Have fun with your child by making up sentences which have several words beginning with the letter **P**. (The pig put a penny in his pocket.)

15

Purpose: To help your child learn the sound associated with the letter **Q** at the beginning of a word.

Directions: 1.   Have your child say the name of each item pictured. Point out that they all begin with the same sound. Have your child say other words which begin the same way. Pronounce some words which begin with **Q** and some which do not and have your child tell you which is which.

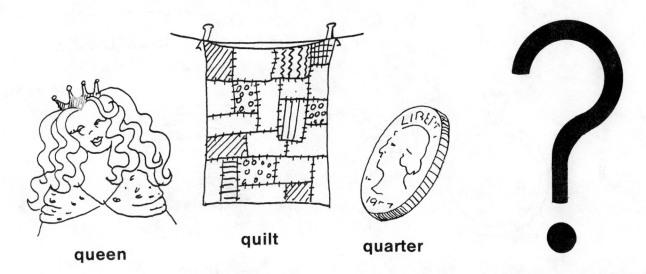

queen   **quilt**   **quarter**

question mark

2.   Have your child look at the name of each item pictured and say it aloud. Point out that the name of each picture begins with the letter **Q** and they all begin with the same sound. Be sure your child understands the sound associated with the letter **Q** at the beginning of a word.

3.   Be certain that your child knows the letter **Q** and can write it. Number several lines on a piece of paper. Pronounce several words which begin with the letter **Q** and some which do not. Have your child write the letter **Q** in the proper space for each word which begins with **Q**. He may leave the other spaces blank.

4.   In magazines or catalogues, let your child find pictures whose names begin with the letter **Q**. He may cut out these pictures and place them in an envelope marked **Q** and use them for further practice. Have fun with your child by making up sentences which have several words beginning with the letter **Q**. (The guiet queen sold a quilt for a quarter.)

16

Purpose: To help your child learn the sound associated with the letter **R** at the beginning of a word.

Directions: 1. Have your child say the name of each item pictured. Point out that they all begin with the same sound. Have your child say other words which begin the same way. Pronounce some words which begin with **R** and some which do not and have your child tell you which is which.

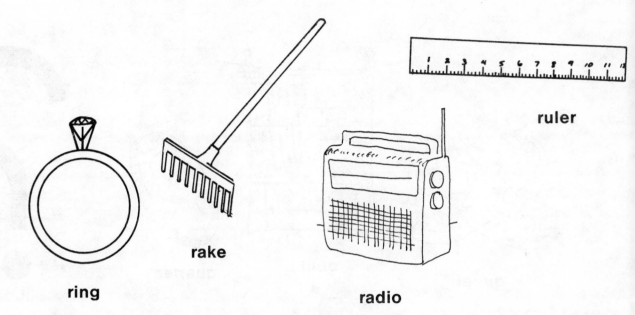

ruler

ring

rake

radio

2. Have your child look at the name of each item pictured and say it aloud. Point out that the name of each picture begins with the letter **R** and they all begin with the same sound. Be sure your child understands the sound associated with the letter **R** at the beginning of a word.

3. Be certain that your child knows the letter **R** and can write it. Number several lines on a piece of paper. Pronounce several words which begin with the letter **R** and some which do not. Have your child write the letter **R** in the proper space for each word which begins with **R**. He may leave the other spaces blank.

4. In magazines or catalogues, let your child find pictures whose names begin with the letter **R**. He may cut out these pictures and place them in an envelope marked **R** and use them for further practice. Have fun with your child by making up sentences which have several words beginning with the letter **R**. (The ring was on the radio.)

17

Purpose: To help your child learn the sound associated with the letter **S** at the beginning of a word.

Directions: 1. Have your child say the name of each item pictured. Point out that they all begin with the same sound. Have your child say other words which begin the same way. Pronounce some words which begin with **S** and some which do not and have your child tell you which is which.

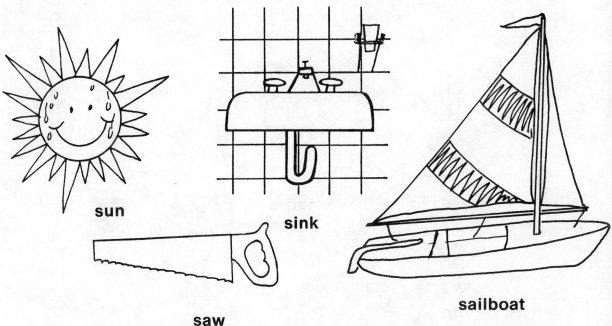

sun

sink

saw

sailboat

2. Have your child look at the name of each item pictured and say it aloud. Point out that the name of each picture begins with the letter **S** and they all begin with the same sound. Be sure your child understands the sound associated with the letter **S** at the beginning of a word.

3. Be certain that your child knows the letter **S** and can write it. Number several lines on a piece of paper. Pronounce several words which begin with the letter **S** and some which do not. Have your child write the letter **S** in the proper space for each word which begins with **S**. He may leave the other spaces blank.

4. In magazines or catalogues, let your child find pictures whose names begin with the letter **S**. He may cut out these pictures and place them in an envelope marked **S** and use them for further practice. Have fun with your child by making up sentences which have several words beginning with the letter **S**. (Sam saw the sail in the sunlight.)

18

Purpose: To help your child learn the sound associated with the letter **T** at the beginning of a word.

Directions: 1. Have your child say the name of each item pictured. Point out that they all begin with the same sound. Have your child say other words which begin the same way. Pronounce some words which begin with **T** and some which do not and have your child tell you which is which.

turtle

television

telephone

top

2. Have your child look at the name of each item pictured and say it aloud. Point out that the name of each picture begins with the letter **T** and they all begin with the same sound. Be sure your child understands the sound associated with the letter **T** at the beginning of a word.

3. Be certain that your child knows the letter **T** and can write it. Number several lines on a piece of paper. Pronounce several words which begin with the letter **T** and some which do not. Have your child write the letter **T** in the proper space for each word which begins with **T**. He may leave the other spaces blank.

4. In magazines or catalogues, let your child find pictures whose names begin with the letter **T**. He may cut out these pictures and place them in an envelope marked **T** and use them for further practice. Have fun with your child by making up sentences which have several words beginning with the letter **T**. (Tell the teacher to talk on the telephone.)

19

Purpose: To help your child learn the sound associated with the letter **V** at the beginning of a word.

Directions: 1.   Have your child say the name of each item pictured. Point out that they all begin with the same sound. Have your child say other words which begin the same way. Pronounce some words which begin with **V** and some which do not and have your child tell you which is which.

violin

vase

valentine

vest

2.   Have your child look at the name of each item pictured and say it aloud. Point out that the name of each picture begins with the letter **V** and they all begin with the same sound. Be sure your child understands the sound associated with the letter **V** at the beginning of a word.

3.   Be certain that your child knows the letter **V** and can write it. Number several lines on a piece of paper. Pronounce several words which begin with the letter **V** and some which do not. Have your child write the letter **V** in the proper space for each word which begins with **V**. He may leave the other spaces blank.

4.   In magazines or catalogues, let your child find pictures whose names begin with the letter **V**. He may cut out these pictures and place them in an envelope marked **V** and use them for further practice. Have fun with your child by making up sentences which have several words beginning with the letter **V**. (Visit your friend and get a very pretty valentine.)

Purpose: To help your child learn the sound associated with the letter **W** at the beginning of a word.

Directions: 1. Have your child say the name of each item pictured. Point out that they all begin with the same sound. Have your child say other words which begin the same way. Pronounce some words which begin with **W** and some which do not and have your child tell you which is which.

window

witch

wagon

watch

2. Have your child look at the name of each item pictured and say it aloud. Point out that the name of each picture begins with the letter **W** and they all begin with the same sound. Be sure your child understands the sound associated with the letter **W** at the beginning of a word.

3. Be certain that your child knows the letter **W** and can write it. Number several lines on a piece of paper. Pronounce several words which begin with the letter **W** and some which do not. Have your child write the letter **W** in the proper space for each word which begins with **W**. He may leave the other spaces blank.

4. In magazines or catalogues, let your child find pictures whose names begin with the letter **W**. He may cut out these pictures and place them in an envelope marked **W** and use them for further practice. Have fun with your child by making up sentences which have several words beginning with the letter **W**. (Will you wait and watch for the wagon to come?)

21

Purpose: To help your child learn the sound associated with the letter **Y** at the beginning of a word.

Directions: 1. Have your child say the name of each item pictured. Point out that they all begin with the same sound. Have your child say other words which begin the same way. Pronounce some words which begin with **Y** and some which do not and have your child tell you which is which.

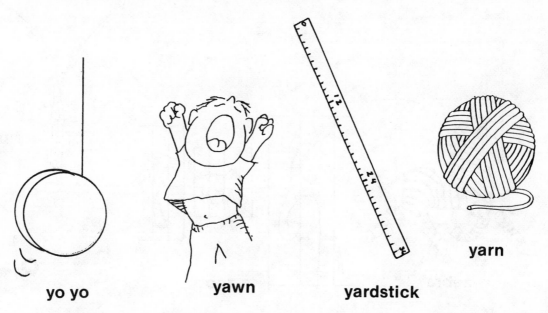

yo yo   **yawn**   **yardstick**   **yarn**

2. Have your child look at the name of each item pictured and say it aloud. Point out that the name of each picture begins with the letter **Y** and they all begin with the same sound. Be sure your child understands the sound associated with the letter **Y** at the beginning of a word.

3. Be certain that your child knows the letter **Y** and can write it. Number several lines on a piece of paper. Pronounce several words which begin with the letter **Y** and some which do not. Have your child write the letter **Y** in the proper space for each word which begins with **Y**. He may leave the other spaces blank.

4. In magazines or catalogues, let your child find pictures whose names begin with the letter **Y**. He may cut out these pictures and place them in an envelope marked **Y** and use them for further practice. Have fun with your child by making up sentences which have several words beginning with the letter **Y**. (You have a yellow yo yo.)

22 Purpose: To help your child learn the sound associated with the letter **Z** at the beginning of a word.

Directions: 1. Have your child say the name of each item pictured. Point out that they all begin with the same sound. Have your child say other words which begin the same way. Pronounce some words which begin with **Z** and some which do not and have your child tell you which is which.

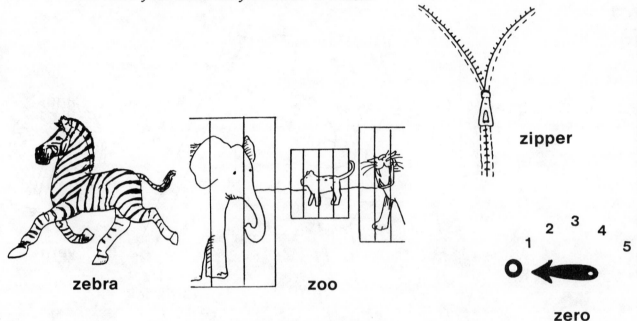

zipper

zebra   **zoo**

zero

2. Have your child look at the name of each item pictured and say it aloud. Point out that the name of each picture begins with the letter **Z** and they all begin with the same sound. Be sure your child understands the sound associated with the letter **Z** at the beginning of a word.

3. Be certain that your child knows the letter **Z** and can write it. Number several lines on a piece of paper. Pronounce several words which begin with the letter **Z** and some which do not. Have your child write the letter **Z** in the proper space for each word which begins with **Z**. He may leave the other spaces blank.

4. In magazines or catalogues, let your child find pictures whose names begin with the letter **Z**. He may cut out these pictures and place them in an envelope marked **Z** and use them for further practice. Have fun with your child by making up sentences which have several words beginning with the letter **Z**. (There is a zebra in the zoo.)

Purpose: To help your child learn the sound associated with the letter **B** at the end of a word.

Directions: 1. Have your child say the name of each item pictured. Point out that they all end with the same sound. Have your child say other words which end the same way. Pronounce some words which end with **B** and some which do not and have your child tell you which is which.

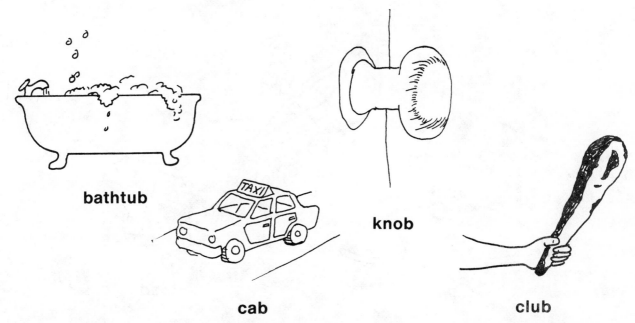

bathtub

cab

knob

club

2. Have your child look at the name of each item pictured and say it aloud. Point out that the name of each picture ends with the letter **B** and they all end with the same sound. Be sure your child understands the sound associated with the letter **B** at the end of a word.

3. Be certain that your child knows the letter **B** and can write it. Number several lines on a piece of paper. Pronounce several words which end with the letter **B** and some which do not. Have your child write the letter **B** in the proper space for each word which ends with **B**. He may leave the other spaces blank.

4. Have your child search through books, papers, or magazines to find words which end with the letter **B**. Help him pronounce the words and notice the sound the letter **B** represents at the end of a word. Have fun with your child by making up sentences which have several words ending with the letter **B**. (Bob saw the web on the tub.)

24

Purpose: To help your child learn the sound associated with the letter **D** at the end of a word.

Directions: 1. Have your child say the name of each item pictured. Point out that they all end with the same sound. Have your child say other words which end the same way. Pronounce some words which end with **D** and some which do not and have your child tell you which is which.

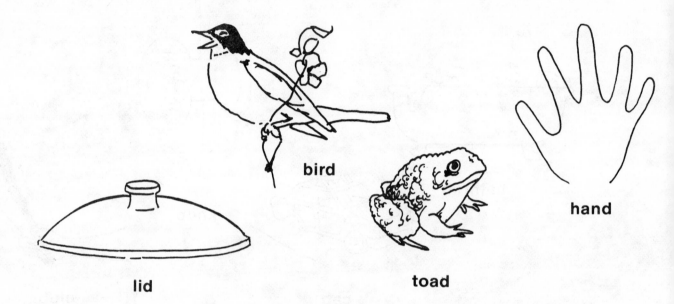

bird

hand

lid

toad

2. Have your child look at the name of each item pictured and say it aloud. Point out that the name of each picture ends with the letter **D** and they all end with the same sound. Be sure your child understands the sound associated with the letter **D** at the end of a word.

3. Be certain that your child knows the letter **D** and can write it. Number several lines on a piece of paper. Pronounce several words which end with the letter **D** and some which do not. Have your child write the letter **D** in the proper space for each word which ends with **D**. He may leave the other spaces blank.

4. Have your child **search through books, papers,** or magazines to find words which end with the letter **D**. Help him pronounce the words and notice the sound the letter **D** represents at the end of a word. Have fun with your child by making up sentences which have several words ending with the letter **D**. (He hid the bread from the bird with his hand.)

Purpose: To help your child learn the sound associated with the letter *F* at the end of a word.

Directions: 1.   Have your child say the name of each item pictured. Point out that they all end with the same sound. Have your child say other words which end the same way. Pronounce some words which end with *F* and some which do not and have your child tell you which is which.

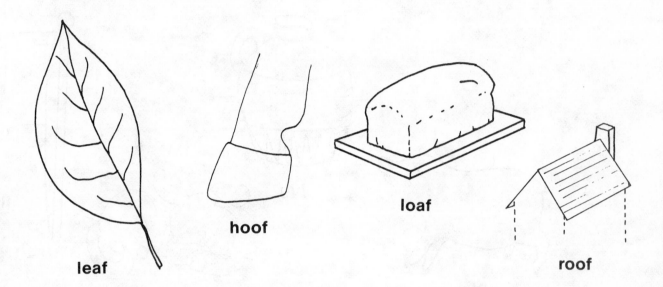

leaf

hoof

loaf

roof

2.   Have your child look at the name of each item pictured and say it aloud. Point out that the name of each picture ends with the letter *F* and they all end with the same sound. Be sure your child understands the sound associated with the letter *F* at the end of a word.

3.   Be certain that your child knows the letter *F* and can write it. Number several lines on a piece of paper. Pronounce several words which end with the letter *F* and some which do not. Have your child write the letter *F* in the proper space for each word which ends with *F*. He may leave the other spaces blank.

4.   Have your child search through books, papers, or magazines to find words which end with the letter *F*. Help him pronounce the words and notice the sound the letter *F* represents at the end of a word. Have fun with your child by making up sentences which have several words ending with the letter *F*. (The calf ate half of the leaf.)

26

Purpose: To help your child learn the sound associated with the letter **G** at the end of a word.

Directions: 1.   Have your child say the name of each item pictured. Point out that they all end with the same sound. Have your child say other words which end the same way. Pronounce some words which end with **G** and some which do not and have your child tell you which is which.

jug

flag

pig

dog

2.   Have your child look at the name of each item pictured and say it aloud. Point out that the name of each picture ends with the letter **G** and they all end with the same sound. Be sure your child understands the sound associated with the letter **G** at the end of a word.

3.   Be certain that your child knows the letter **G** and can write it. Number several lines on a piece of paper. Pronounce several words which end with the letter **G** and some which do not. Have your child write the letter **G** in the proper space for each word which ends with **G**. He may leave the other spaces blank.

4.   Have your child search through books, papers, or magazines to find words which end with the letter **G**. Help him pronounce the words and notice the sound the letter **G** represents at the end of a word. Have fun with your child by making up sentences which have several words ending with the letter **G**. (The dog and the pig wore a wig.)

 **Purpose:** To help your child learn the sound associated with the letter **K** at the end of a word.

Directions: 1. Have your child say the name of each item pictured. Point out that they all end with the same sound. Have your child say other words which end the same way. Pronounce some words which end with **K** and some which do not and have your child tell you which is which.

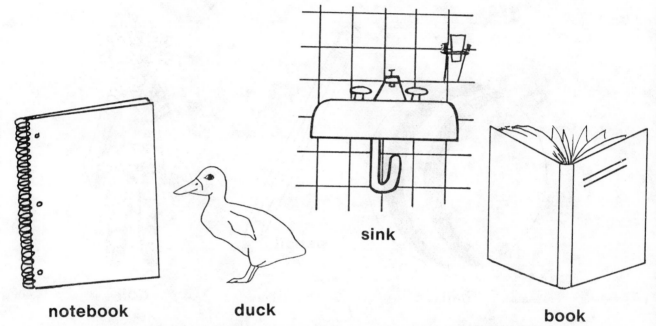

notebook   **duck**   **sink**   **book**

2. Have your child look at the name of each item pictured and say it aloud. Point out that the name of each picture ends with the letter **K** and they all end with the same sound. Be sure your child understands the sound associated with the letter **K** at the end of a word.

3. Be certain that your child knows the letter **K** and can write it. Number several lines on a piece of paper. Pronounce several words which end with the letter **K** and some which do not. Have your child write the letter **K** in the proper space for each word which ends with **K**. He may leave the other spaces blank.

4. Have your child search through books, papers, or magazines to find words which end with the letter **K**. Help him pronounce the words and notice the sound the letter **K** represents at the end of a word. Have fun with your child by making up sentences which have several words ending with the letter **K**. (He took a look at the book.)

Purpose: To help your child learn the sound associated with the letter **L** at the end of a word.

Directions: 1.   Have your child say the name of each item pictured. Point out that they all end with the same sound. Have your child say other words which end the same way. Pronounce some words which end with **L** and some which do not and have your child tell you which is which.

ball

pencil

doll

nail

2.   Have your child look at the name of each item pictured and say it aloud. Point out that the name of each picture ends with the letter **L** and they all end with the same sound. Be sure your child understands the sound associated with the letter **L** at the end of a word.

3.   Be certain that your child knows the letter **L** and can write it. Number several lines on a piece of paper. Pronounce several words which end with the letter **L** and some which do not. Have your child write the letter **L** in the proper space for each word which ends with **L**. He may leave the other spaces blank.

4.   Have your child search through books, papers, or magazines to find words which end with the letter **L**. Help him pronounce the words and notice the sound the letter **L** represents at the end of a word. Have fun with your child by making up sentences which have several words ending with the letter **L**. (Nell will tell Will all about it.)

Purpose: To help your child learn the sound associated with the letter **M** at the end of a word.

Directions: 1.   Have your child say the name of each item pictured. Point out that they all end with the same sound. Have your child say other words which end the same way. Pronounce some words which end with **M** and some which do not and have your child tell you which is which.

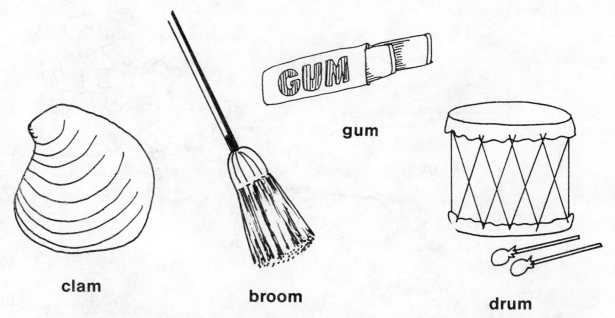

clam   **broom**   **drum**

gum

2.   Have your child look at the name of each item pictured and say it aloud. Point out that the name of each picture ends with the letter **M** and they all end with the same sound. Be sure your child understands the sound associated with the letter **M** at the end of a word.

3.   Be certain that your child knows the letter **M** and can write it. Number several lines on a piece of paper. Pronounce several words which end with the letter **M** and some which do not. Have your child write the letter **M** in the proper space for each word which ends with **M**. He may leave the other spaces blank.

4.   Have your child search through books, papers, or magazines to find words which end with the letter **M**. Help him pronounce the words and notice the sound the letter **M** represents at the end of a word. Have fun with your child by making up sentences which have several words ending with the letter **M**. (Tom got gum on his drum.)

30

Purpose: To help your child learn the sound associated with the letter **N** at the end of a word.

Directions: 1. Have your child say the name of each item pictured. Point out that they all end with the same sound. Have your child say other words which end the same way. Pronounce some words which end with **N** and some which do not and have your child tell you which is which.

gun

queen

lion

kitten

2. Have your child look at the name of each item pictured and say it aloud. Point out that the name of each picture ends with the letter **N** and they all end with the same sound. Be sure your child understands the sound associated with the letter **N** at the end of a word.

3. Be certain that your child knows the letter **N** and can write it. Number several lines on a piece of paper. Pronounce several words which end with the letter **N** and some which do not. Have your child write the letter **N** in the proper space for each word which ends with **N**. He may leave the other spaces blank.

4. Have your child search through books, papers, or magazines to find words which end with the letter **N**. Help him pronounce the words and notice the sound the letter **N** represents at the end of a word. Have fun with your child by making up sentences which have several words ending with the letter **N**. (The queen saw the lion in his den.)

31

Purpose: To help your child learn the sound associated with the letter **P** at the end of a word.

Directions: 1. Have your child say the name of each item pictured. Point out that they all end with the same sound. Have your child say other words which end the same way. Pronounce some words which end with **P** and some which do not and have your child tell you which is which.

top

mop

jeep

cup

2.   Have your child look at the name of each item pictured and say it aloud. Point out that the name of each picture ends with the letter **P** and they all end with the same sound. Be sure your child understands the sound associated with the letter **P** at the end of a word.

3.   Be certain that your child knows the letter **P** and can write it. Number several lines on a piece of paper. Pronounce several words which end with the letter **P** and some which do not. Have your child write the letter **P** in the proper space for each word which ends with **P**. He may leave the other spaces blank.

4.   Have your child search through books, papers, or magazines to find words which end with the letter **P**. Help him pronounce the words and notice the sound the letter **P** represents at the end of a word. Have fun with your child by making up sentences which have several words ending with the letter **P**. (The cop will hop in the jeep and stop robbers.)

32

Purpose: To help your child learn the sound associated with the letter **R** at the end of a word.

Directions: 1.   Have your child say the name of each item pictured. Point out that they all end with the same sound. Have your child say other words which end the same way. Pronounce some words which end with **R** and some which do not and have your child tell you which is which.

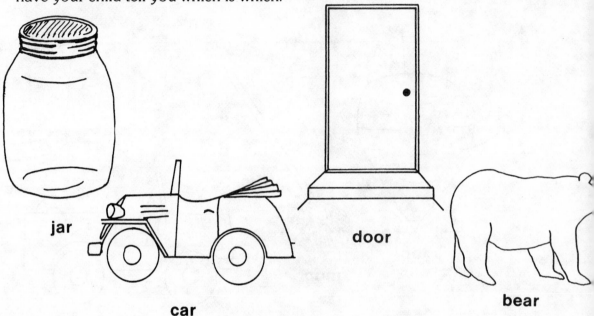

jar

car

door

bear

2.   Have your child look at the name of each item pictured and say it aloud. Point out that the name of each picture ends with the letter **R** and they all end with the same sound. Be sure your child understands the sound associated with the letter **R** at the end of a word.

3.   Be certain that your child knows the letter **R** and can write it. Number several lines on a piece of paper. Pronounce several words which end with the letter **R** and some which do not. Have your child write the letter **R** in the proper space for each word which ends with **R**. He may leave the other spaces blank.

4.   Have your child **search through books, papers, or magazines to find words** which end with the letter **R**. Help him pronounce the words and notice the sound the letter **R** represents at the end of a word. Have fun with your child by making up sentences which have several words ending with the letter **R**. (Father put the bear and the deer in the car.)

33

Purpose: To help your child learn the sound associated with the letter **S** at the end of a word.

Directions: 1. Have your child say the name of each item pictured. Point out that they all end with the same sound. Have your child say other words which end the same way. Pronounce some words which end with **S** and some which do not and have your child tell you which is which.

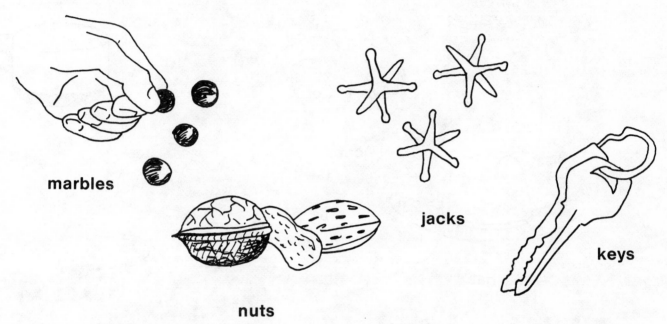

marbles

jacks

keys

nuts

2. Have your child look at the name of each item pictured and say it aloud. Point out that the name of each picture ends with the letter **S** and they all end with the same sound. Be sure your child understands the sound associated with the letter **S** at the end of a word.

3. Be certain that your child knows the letter **S** and can write it. Number several lines on a piece of paper. Pronounce several words which end with the letter **S** and some which do not. Have your child write the letter **S** in the proper space for each word which ends with **S**. He may leave the other spaces blank.

4. Have your child **search through books, papers**, or magazines to find words which end with the letter **S**. Help him pronounce the words and notice the sound the letter **S** represents at the end of a word. Have fun with your child by making up sentences which have **several words ending** with the letter **S**. (Gus put gas in the bus.)

34

Purpose: To help your child learn the sound associated with the letter **T** at the end of a word.

Directions: 1.   Have your child say the name of each item pictured. Point out that they all end with the same sound. Have your child say other words which end the same way. Pronounce some words which end with **T** and some which do not and have your child tell you which is which.

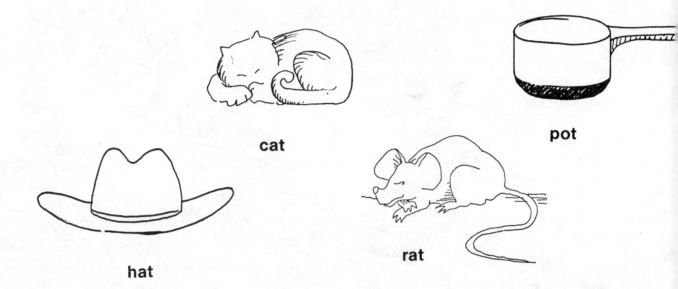

cat

pot

hat

rat

2.   Have your child look at the name of each item pictured and say it aloud. Point out that the name of each picture ends with the letter **T** and they all end with the same sound. Be sure your child understands the sound associated with the letter **T** at the end of a word.

3.   Be certain that your child knows the letter **T** and can write it. Number several lines on a piece of paper. Pronounce several words which end with the letter **T** and some which do not. Have your child write the letter **T** in the proper space for each word which ends with **T**. He may leave the other spaces blank.

4.   Have your child search through books, papers, or magazines to find words which end with the letter **T**. Help him pronounce the words and notice the sound the letter **T** represents at the end of a word. Have fun with your child by making up sentences which have several words ending with the letter **T**. (The fat cat sat on the mat.)

35

Purpose: To help your child learn the sound associated with the letter **X** at the end of a word.

Directions: 1.   Have your child say the name of each item pictured. Point out that they all end with the same sound. Have your child say other words which end the same way. Pronounce some words which end with **X** and some which do not and have your child tell you which is which.

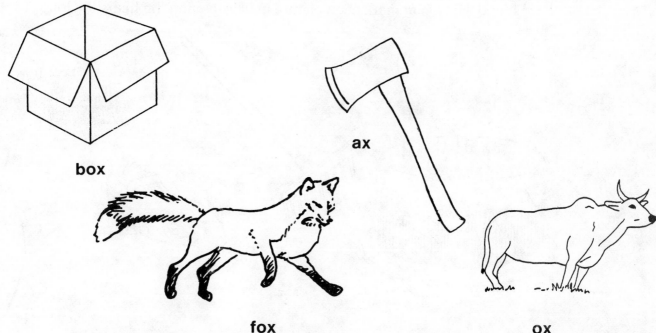

box

ax

fox

ox

2.   Have your child look at the name of each item pictured and say it aloud. Point out that the name of each picture ends with the letter **X** and they all end with the same sound. Be sure your child understands the sound associated with the letter **X** at the end of a word.

3.   Be certain that your child knows the letter **X** and can write it. Number several lines on a piece of paper. Pronounce several words which end with the letter **X** and some which do not. Have your child write the letter **X** in the proper space for each word which ends with **X**. He may leave the other spaces blank.

4.   Have your child search through books, papers, or magazines to find words which end with the letter **X**. Help him pronounce the words and notice the sound the letter **X** represents at the end of a word. Have fun with your child by making up sentences which have several words ending with the letter **X**. (The ox was in the box with the fox.)

36

Purpose: To help your child learn the long sound of the vowel **A**.

Directions: 1. Help your child understand that the long sound of the vowel **A** is the sound you hear when you say the name of the letter **A**. It is the vowel sound heard in **make, rake, steak,** and **take**. Have your child say other words which have the long **A** vowel sound.

2. Help your child say the name of each item pictured and listen for the vowel sound. Have him mark each picture in whose name he hears the long **A** sound.

3. Pronounce some words which have the long **A** vowel sound and some which do not. Have your child listen to the words and tell you which have the long **A** vowel sound and which do not.

4. In magazines or catalogues, help your child find pictures whose names have the long **A** vowel sound. Have him say the name of each picture and listen for the long **A** vowel sound. He may wish to cut out the pictures, place them in an envelope marked "Long **A**" and use them for further practice.

5. Have fun with your child by making up sentences in which there are several words which have the long **A** vowel sound. They may be nonsense, just for fun. (Today we may play in the hay.)

37

Purpose: To help your child learn the long sound of the vowel *E*.

Directions: 1. Help your child understand that the long sound of the vowel *E* is the sound you hear when you say the name of the letter *E*. It is the vowel sound heard in **sea, meat, leaf,** and **key**. Have your child say other words which have the long *E* vowel sound.

2. Help your child say the name of each item pictured and listen for the vowel sound. Have him mark each picture in whose name he hears the long *E* sound.

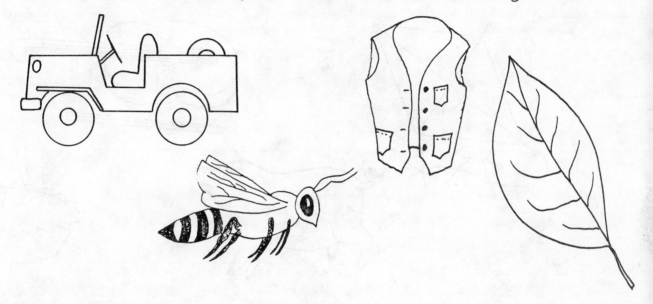

3. Pronounce some words which have the long *E* vowel sound and some which do not. Have your child listen to the words and tell you which have the long *E* vowel sound and which do not.

4. In magazines or catalogues, help your child find pictures whose names have the long *E* vowel sound. Have him say the name of each picture and listen for the long *E* vowel sound. He may wish to cut out the pictures, place them in an envelope marked "Long *E*" and use them for further practice.

5. Have fun with your child by making up sentences in which there are several words which have the long *E* vowel sound. They may be nonsense, just for fun. (I would rather see an eel than feel an eel.)

Purpose: To help your child learn the long sound of the vowel *I*.

Directions: 1.   Help your child understand that the long sound of the vowel *I* is the sound you hear when you say the name of the letter *I*. It is the vowel sound heard in *mice, kite, light,* and *rice.* Have your child say other words which have the long *I* vowel sound.

2.   Help your child say the name of each item pictured and listen for the vowel sound. Have him mark each picture in whose name he hears the long *I* sound.

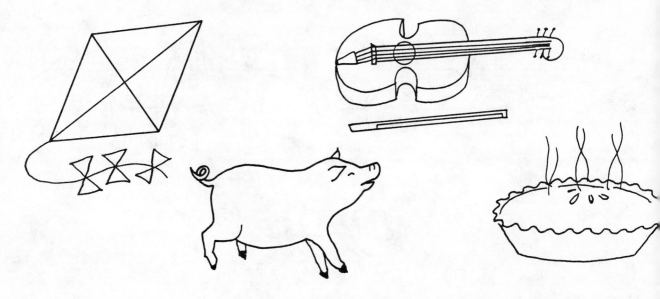

3.   Pronounce some words which have the long *I* vowel sound and some which do not. Have your child listen to the words and tell you which have the long *I* vowel sound and which do not.

4.   In magazines or catalogues, help your child find pictures whose names have the long *I* vowel sound. Have him say the name of each picture and listen for the long *I* vowel sound. He may wish to cut out the pictures, place them in an envelope marked "Long *I*" and use them for further practice.

5.   Have fun with your child by making up sentences in which there are several words which have the long *I* vowel sound. They may be nonsense, just for fun. (I will ride a lion in the night.)

39

Purpose: To help your child learn the long sound of the vowel **O**.

Directions: 1.   Help your child understand that the long sound of the vowel **O** is the sound you hear when you say the name of the letter **O**. It is the vowel sound heard in **boat, go, float,** and **low**. Have your child say other words which have the long **O** vowel sound.

2.   Help your child say the name of each item pictured and listen for the vowel sound. Have him mark each picture in whose name he hears the long **O** sound.

3.   Pronounce some words which have the long **O** vowel sound and some which do not. Have your child listen to the words and tell you which have the long **O** vowel sound and which do not.

4.   In magazines or catalogues, help your child find pictures whose names have the long **O** vowel sound. Have him say the name of each picture and listen for the long **O** vowel sound. He may wish to cut out the pictures, place them in an envelope marked "Long **O**" and use them for further practice.

5.   Have fun with your child by making up sentences in which there are several words which have the long **O** vowel sound. They may be nonsense, just for fun. (Go put the goat in the boat.)

Purpose: To help your child learn the long sound of the vowel **U**.

Directions: 1.   Help your child understand that the long sound of the vowel **U** is the sound you hear when you say the name of the letter **U**. It is the vowel sound heard in **mule, rule, tube,** and **use**. Have your child say other words which have the long **U** vowel sound.

2.   Help your child say the name of each item pictured and listen for the vowel sound. Have him mark each picture in whose name he hears the long **U** sound.

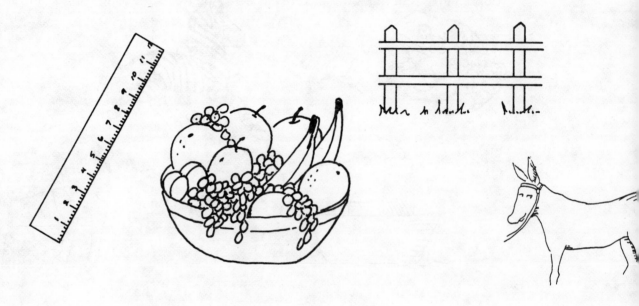

3.   Pronounce some words which have the long **U** vowel sound and some which do not. Have your child listen to the words and tell you which have the long **U** vowel sound and which do not.

4.   In magazines or catalogues, help your child find pictures whose names have the long **U** vowel sound. Have him say the name of each picture and listen for the long **U** vowel sound. He may wish to cut out the pictures, place them in an envelope marked "Long **U**" and use them for further practice.

5.   Have fun with your child by making up sentences in which there are several words which have the long **U** vowel sound. They may be nonsense, just for fun. (The mule knew the rule.)

Purpose: To help your child with the sound of the letter **Y** when it is used as a vowel in a word.

Direction: 1. Help your child understand that the long sound of the letter **Y**, when it is used as a vowel, is the sound you hear when you say the name of the letter **Y**. It is the vowel sound you hear in **dry, try,** and **shy**. Help your child think of other words in which this sound is heard (**fly, my, by, buy, spy, sly**).

2. Help your child say the name of each item pictured and listen for the vowel sound. Have him mark the pictures in which he hears the long sound of the vowel **Y**.

3. Pronounce some words which have the long **Y** sound and some which do not. Have your child listen to the words and tell you which have the long **Y** sound and which do not.

4. Help your child read these words and listen for the sound of **Y** at the end of each. Have him draw a line under each word in which **Y** sounds like the **Y** in **cry**.

fly   baby   puppy   buy   sly   my

5. Have fun with your child by making up sentences in which there are several words which have the long **Y** sound. They may be nonsense, just for fun. (Why did the spy try to fly?)

 **Purpose:** To help your child learn the short sound of the vowel **A**.

Directions: 1.   Help your child understand that the short sound of the vowel **A** is the sound you hear when you say *cat, flag,* and *glass.* Help your child say other words which have the short **A** vowel sound *(apple, taxi, matches, cap, hatchet, tack,* etc.)

2.   Help your child say the name of each item pictured and listen for the vowel sound. Have him mark each picture in whose name he hears the short sound of **A**.

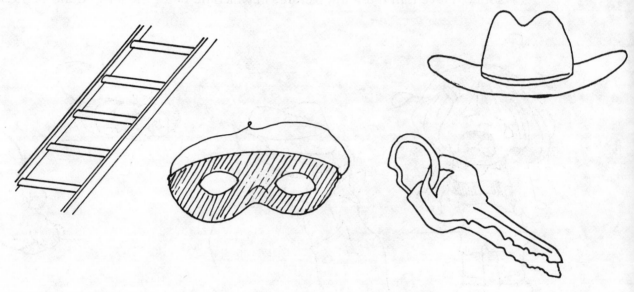

3.   Pronounce some words which have a short **A** sound and some which do not. Have your child tell you which is which.

4.   In magazines or catalogues, help your child find pictures whose names have the short **A** vowel sound. He may cut out these pictures and place them in an envelope marked "Short **A**" and use them for further practice.

5.   Have fun with your child by making up sentences in which there are several words which have the short **A** vowel sound. They may be nonsense, just for fun. (The cat put the flag in the glass.)

Purpose: To help your child learn the short sound of the vowel *E*.

Directions: 1.   Help your child understand that the short sound of the vowel *E* is the sound you hear when you say **pet, bell, sled** and **red.** Help your child say other words which have the short *E* vowel sound (**belt, net, dress, neck, bed, hen, eggs,** etc.)

2.   Help your child say the name of each item pictured and listen for the vowel sound. Have him mark each picture in whose name he hears the short sound of *E*.

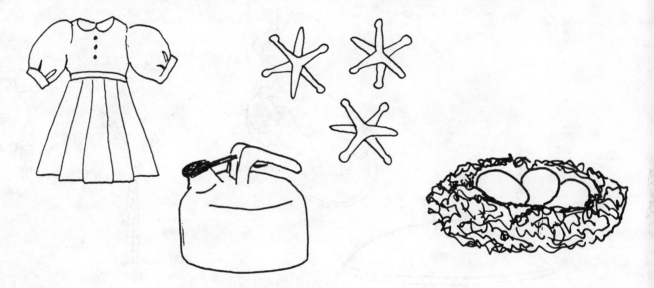

3.   Pronounce some words which have a short *E* sound and some which do not. Have your child tell you which is which.

4.   In magazines or catalogues, help your child find pictures whose names have the short *E* vowel sound. He may cut out these pictures and place them in an envelope marked "Short *E*" and use them for further practice.

5.   Have fun with your child by making up sentences in which there are several words which have the short *E* vowel sound. They may be nonsense, just for fun. (There was a bell on the red sled.)

 **Purpose:** To help your child learn the short sound of the vowel **I**.

Directions: 1. Help your child understand that the short sound of the vowel **I** is the sound you hear when you say **milk, kittens, ship, fish** and **pin.** Help your child say other words which have the short **I** vowel sound (**did, mittens, pillow, sit, pig, him, win, lip,** etc.)

2. Help your child say the name of each item pictured and listen for the vowel sound. Have him mark each picture in whose name he hears the short sound of **I**.

3. Pronounce some words which have a short **I** sound and some which do not. Have your child tell you which is which.

4. In magazines or catalogues, help your child find pictures whose names have the short **I** vowel sound. He may cut out these pictures and place them in an envelope marked "Short **I**" and use them for further practice.

5. Have fun with your child by making up sentences in which there are several words which have the short **I** vowel sound. They may be nonsense, just for fun. (The kittens and the pig sit on the pillow.)

Purpose: To help your child learn the short sound of the vowel **O**.

Directions: 1.   Help your child understand that the short sound of the vowel **O** is the sound you hear when you say **doll, shop, rocks** and **socks.** Help your child say other words which have the short **O** vowel sound (**not, chop, dot, hop, stop,** etc.)

2.   Help your child say the name of each item pictured and listen for the vowel sound. Have him mark each picture in whose name he hears the short sound of **O**.

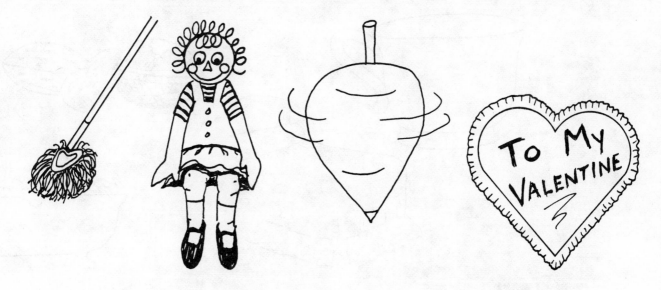

3.   Pronounce some words which have a short **O** sound and some which do not. Have your child tell you which is which.

4.   In magazines or catalogues, help your child find pictures whose names have the short **O** vowel sound. He may cut out these pictures and place them in an envelope marked "Short **O**" and use them for further practice.

5.   Have fun with your child by making up sentences in which there are several words which have the short **O** vowel sound. They may be nonsense, just for fun. (Do not put the rocks in the pot.)

Purpose: To help your child learn the short sound of the vowel **U**.

Directions: 1.   Help your child understand that the short sound of the vowel **U** is the sound you hear when you say *dug, gun, shut* and *bus.* Help your child say other words which have the short **U** vowel sound *(us, gum, run, fun, ducks, drum, much,* etc.)

2.   Help your child say the name of each item pictured and listen for the vowel sound. Have him mark each picture in whose name he hears the short sound of **U**.

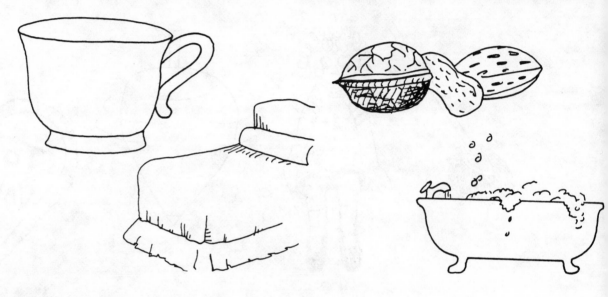

3.   Pronounce some words which have a short **U** sound and some which do not. Have your child tell you which is which.

4.   In magazines or catalogues, help your child find pictures whose names have the short **U** vowel sound. He may cut out these pictures and place them in an envelope marked "Short **U**" and use them for further practice.

5.   Have fun with your child by making up sentences in which there are several words which have the short **U** vowel sound. They may be nonsense, just for fun. (The ducks had fun with the drum.)

Purpose: To help your child with the short sound of the letter **Y** when it is used as a vowel in a word.

Directions: 1.   Help your child understand that the short sound of the letter **Y**, when it is used as a vowel in a word, is the sound you hear in **baby, happy, many,** and **story.** Help your child think of other words in which the short sound of the vowel **Y** is heard **(any, candy, penny, funny.)**
2.   Help your child say the name of each item pictured and listen for the sound of the vowel **Y**. Have him mark the pictures in which he hears the short sound of **Y**.

3.   Pronounce some words which have the short **Y** sound and some which do not. Have your child listen to the words and tell you which has the short **Y** sound and which does not.
4.   Help your child read these words and listen for the sound of **Y** at the end of each. Have him draw a line under each word in which **Y** sounds like **Y** in **baby.**

cry   penny   funny   spy   candy   any

5.   Have fun with your child by making up sentences in which there are several words which have the long **Y** sound. They may be nonsense, just for fun. (The happy baby got some candy for a penny.)

ut the picture cards and use them in a variety of ways:

Put together the cards containing picture whose names begin with the same sound, or some sound you select.

2. Put together the cards containing pictures whose names end with the same sound, or some sound you select.

3. Put together the cards containing pictures whose names rhyme.

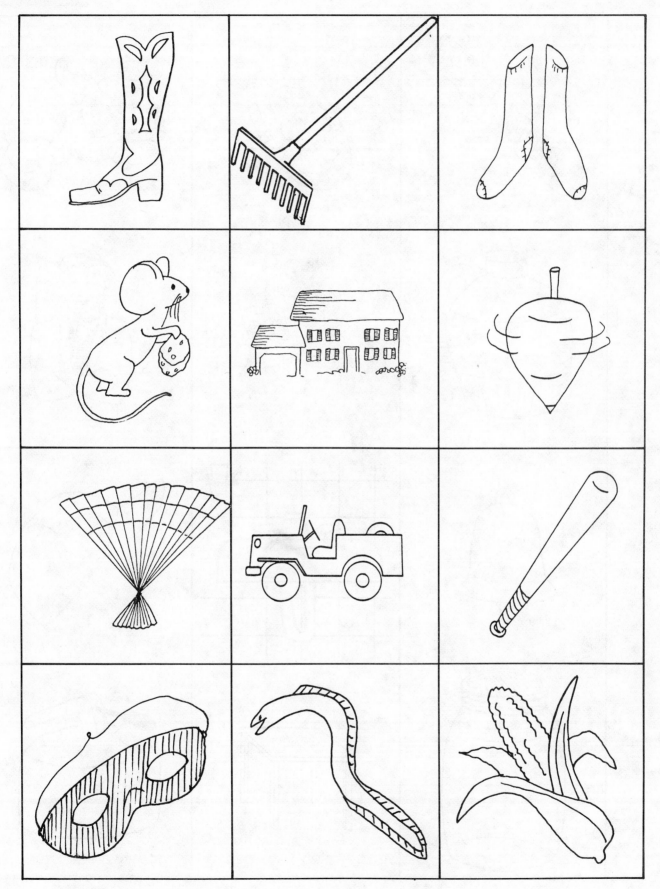

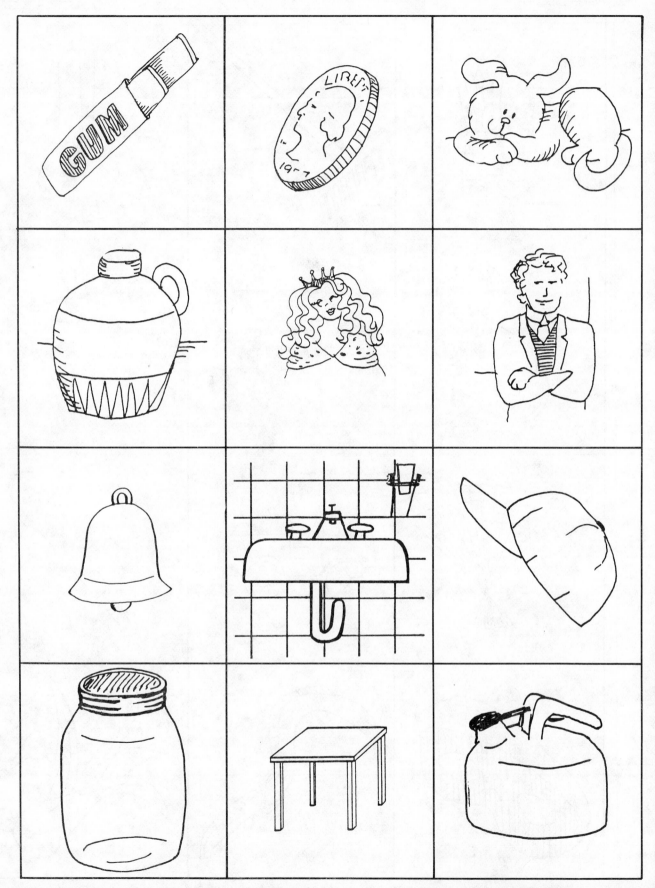

MILK

Start 1	 2	 3
  4	**Skip two spaces** 5	 6
  7	 8	**Miss the next turn** 9
Go back two spaces 10	 11	 12
  13	**Take an extra turn** 14	 15
  16	 17	**THE WINNER!** 18

Game Variations To Use With Game Board

If your family has a spinner or dice from a game of chance, use them to determine how many moves to make on the game board. Use any small objects you wish for tokens. You don't need a spinner or dice, however, to play these games. The players may take turns and simply move one space each turn, unless the instructions direct the player to do otherwise.

There are many variations to this game. Your child's teacher will probably indicate which one he/she thinks will be best for your child to play.

1.   Each player may move his/her token the indicated number of spaces if he/she can say the required number of words (1,2,3 or more, agreed upon before the game begins) beginning with a consonant sound which you have chosen to work on.

2.   Each player may move his/her token the indicated number of spaces if he/she can say the required number of words (1,2,3 or more, agreed upon before the game begins) which rhyme with each other.

3.   Each player may move his/her token the indicated number of spaces if he/she can say the required number of words (1,2,3 or more, agreed upon before the game begins) which end with a consonant sound which you have chosen to work on.

Purpose: To help your child review the sound associated with letters at the beginning of words.

Directions: 1. Help your child say the name of each item pictured and listen for the sound represented by the first letter. If you are studying a particular letter, help your child write that letter under all pictures whose names begin with that letter. For example, if you are studying *B*, have your child write *B* under all pictures whose names begin with *B*.

2. For review, help your child say the name of each item pictured and write under each picture the first letter in the name of that item.

Purpose: To help your child review the sounds associated with consonants at the end of words.

Directions: 1.   Help your child say the name of each item pictured and listen for the final sound in each. If you are reviewing a particular letter, help your child write that letter under all pictures whose names end with the sound that letter represents. For example, if you are reviewing the letter *B*, have your child write *B* under all pictures whose names end with the sound of the letter *B*.
2.   For review, help your child say the name of each item pictured and write under each picture the letter which represents the last sound in the name of that item.

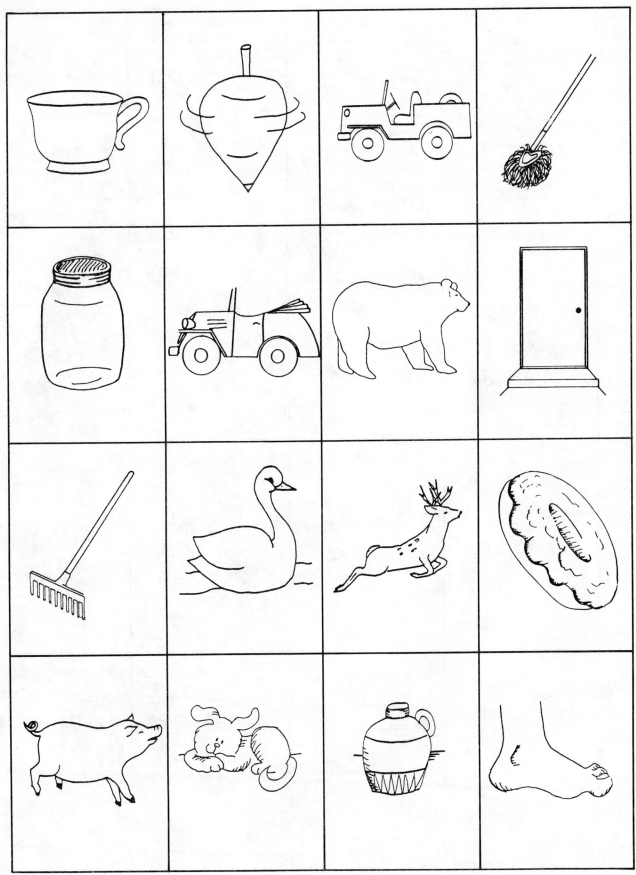

Purpose: To give your child practice in recognizing long and short sounds in words.

Directions: 1. Help your child understand that when you mark a vowel to show whether it has a long or short sound, long vowels are marked like this: cāke, kēy, kīte, gōat, and rūler. Short vowels are marked like this: hăt, věst, fĭsh, dŏll, and cŭp.

2. Help your child look at these pictures and say the name of each one. Help him decide whether the first vowel in each word has a long or short vowel sound. Help him mark the first vowel as a long or short sound.

eel	tractor	net	log
milk	notebook	table	deer
fish	zebra	ox	top
keys	kite	hat	ghost
bed	vest	cake	ruler

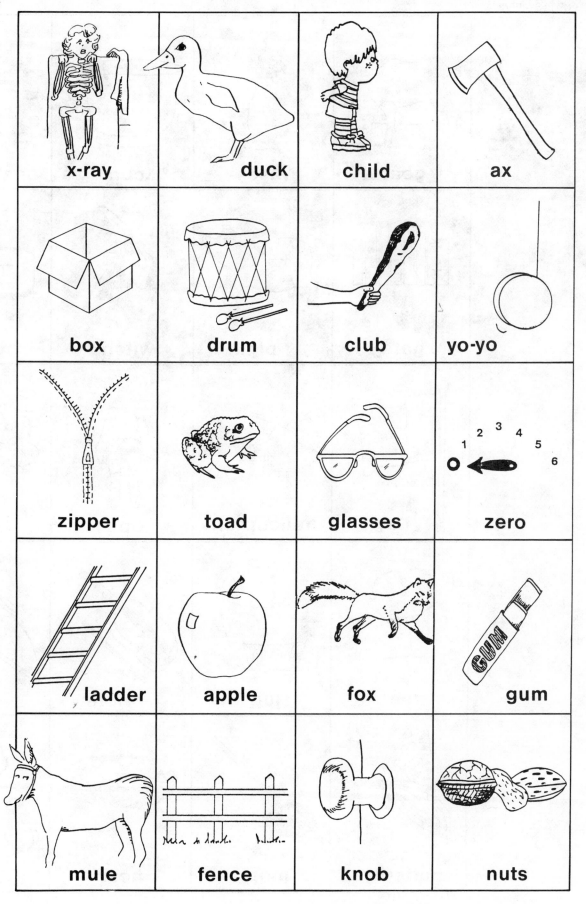

x-ray	duck	child	ax
box	drum	club	yo-yo
zipper	toad	glasses	zero
ladder	apple	fox	gum
mule	fence	knob	nuts

157

goat	vase	cup	nail
gate	pig	witch	pot
flag	helicopter	doll	dog
tree	jug	violin	lid
butterfly	mop	nest	baby

 To make a sound-blending device, cut along the heavy black lines. Fold on the dotted lines and paste or tape flaps together in back to make an envelope. Insert the letter strip into the long envelope and position it so that the letters appear in the windows. Blend sounds of letters with word endings to make real or nonsense words.

ake
ate
et
old
ook
ot
own
all
ain
ail

b
c
d
f
g
h
j
k
l
m
n
p
q
r
s
t
v
w
x
y
z

To make a sound-blending device, cut along the heavy black lines. Fold on the dotted lines and paste or tape flaps together in back to make an envelope. Insert the letter strip into the long envelope and position it so that the letters appear in the windows. Blend sounds of letters with word endings to make real or nonsense words.

☐	ing
☐	ill
☐	ack
☐	at
☐	ell
☐	ip
☐	ap
☐	op
☐	ame
☐	ed

b
c
d
f
g
h
j
k
l
m
n
p
q
r
s
t
v
w
x
y
z

Purpose: To help your child review the sounds associated with the letter *C* at the beginning of a word.

Directions: All the following words begin with the letter *C*. In some words, the letter *C* has a *K* sound, as in the words *camp* and *coat.* In other words the letter *C* has an *S* sound as in the words *circle* and *center.* Help your child read these words and listen for the sound of the letter *C* in each. Help him write the words in which *C* has its *K* sound under the picture of a comb. Have him write the words in which *C* has its *S* sound under the picture of a cigar.

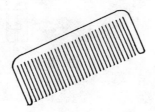

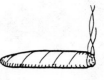

cigar

coat

cent

camp

come

city

circle

coin

cave

cell

cap

cold

cow

cellar

Purpose: To help your child review the sounds associated with the letter **G** in words.

Directions: In some words, the letter **G** represents its hard sound as heard in words like **go, get, give,** and **game.** In other words the letter **G** represents its soft or **J** sound as heard in **gym, gypsy,** and **germ.** Help your child read these words and listen for the sound of the letter **G** in each. Help him write the words in which the letter **G** has its hard sound under the picture of a gate. Help him write the words in which the letter **G** has its soft or **J** sound under the picture of a giraffe.

girl

giant

beg

gentle

age

drag

game

page

engine

gag

germ

ginger

gang

gap

gas

gym

gypsy

get

The Successful Teacher's Most Valuable Resource!

EDUCATION

THE EARLI PROGRAM
Excellent language development program! Volume I contains developmentally sequenced lessons in verbal receptive language; Volume II, expressive language. Use as a primary, supplemental or rehabilitative language program.

Volume I	No. 067-7	**$14.95**
Volume II	No. 074-X	**$14.95**

LEARNING ENVIRONMENTS FOR CHILDREN
A practical manual for creating efficient, pleasant and stress-free learning environments for children centers. Make the best possible use of your center's space!

No. 065-0   **$12.95**

COMPETENCIES:
A Self-Study Guide to Teaching Competencies in Early Childhood Education

This comprehensive guide is ideal for evaluating or improving your competency in early childhood education or preparing for the CDA credential.

No. 024-3   **$12.95**

LOOKING AT CHILDREN:
Field Experiences in Child Study

A series of fourteen units made up of structured exercises dealing with such issues as language development, play and moral development in children. A fresh new approach to learning materials for early childhood educators.

No. 001-4   **$12.95**

YOUNG CHILDREN'S BEHAVIOR:
Implementing Your Goals

A variety of up-to-date approaches to discipline and guidance to help you deal more effectively with children. Also an excellent addition to CDA and competency-based training programs.

No. 015-4   **$7.95**

NUTS AND BOLTS
The ultimate guide to classroom organization and management of an early learning environment. Provides complete guidelines for setting up an early learning center; also excellent for improving an existing school system.

No. 063-4   **$6.95**

READING ROOTS:
Teach Your Child

Teach your child a basic reading vocabulary centered around the colors of his crayons before he enters school. Enjoyable coloring and matching activities make learning to read fun for both you and your child.

No. 070-7   **$10.95**

BACK TO BASICS IN READING MADE FUN
Refreshing and innovative approach to teaching basic reading skills which will delight and stimulate students. Over 100 creative games and projects to use in designing exciting reading materials.

No. 060-X   **$12.95**

ACTIVITY BOOKS

EARLY CHILDHOOD ACTIVITIES:
A Treasury of Ideas from Worldwide Sources

A virtual encyclopedia of projects, games and activities for children aged 3 to 7, containing over 500 different child-tested activities drawn from a variety of teaching systems. The ultimate activity book!

No. 066-9   **$16.95**

VANILLA MANILA FOLDER GAMES
Make exciting and stimulating Vanilla Manila Folder Games quickly and easily with simple manila file folders and colored marking pens. Unique learning activities designed for children aged 3 to 8.

No. 059-6   **$14.95**

HANDBOOK OF LEARNING ACTIVITIES
Over 125 exciting, enjoyable activities and projects for young children in the areas of math, health and safety, play, movement, science, social studies, art, language development, puppetry and more!

No. 058-8   **$14.95**

MONTH BY MONTH ACTIVITY GUIDE FOR THE PRIMARY GRADES
Month by Month gives you a succinct guide to the effective recruitment and utilization of teachers' aides plus a full year's worth of fun-filled educational activities in such areas as reading, math, art, and science.

No. 061-8   **$14.95**

ART PROJECTS FOR YOUNG CHILDREN
Build a basic art program of stimulating projects on a limited budget and time schedule with Art Projects. Contains over 100 fun-filled projects in the areas of drawing, painting, puppets, clay, printing and more!

No. 051-0   **$12.95**

AEROSPACE PROJECTS FOR YOUNG CHILDREN
Introduce children to the fascinating field of aerospace with the exciting and informative projects and field trip suggestions. Contributors include over 30 aviation/aerospace agencies and personnel.

No. 052-9   **$12.95**

CHILD'S PLAY:
An Activities and Materials Handbook

An eclectic selection of fun-filled activities for preschool children designed to lend excitement to the learning process. Activities include puppets, mobiles, poetry, songs and more.

No. 003-0   **$12.95**

ENERGY:
A Curriculum for 3, 4 and 5 Year Olds

Help preschool children become aware of what energy is, the sources of energy, the uses of energy and wise energy use with the fun-filled activities, songs and games included in this innovative manual.

No. 069-3   **$9.95**

Humanics Publications

PARENT INVOLVEMENT

LOVE NOTES
A one year's supply of ready-to-use "Love Notes" to send home with the child to the parent. A novel and charming way to help parents enrich their parenting skills.
No. 068-5   **$19.95**

WORKING PARENTS:
How To Be Happy With Your Children
Dozens of easy and effective techniques and activities which will promote a constructive and enjoyable home and family life for the child and the working parent.
No. 006-5   **$7.95**

WORKING TOGETHER:
A Guide To Parent Involvement
Ideal guide for those wishing to launch a new parent involvement program or improve existing parent/school communication and interaction. Favorably reviewed by the National Association for Education of Young Children.
No. 003-0   **$12.95**

PARENTS AND TEACHERS
An intelligent, effective and field-tested program for improving the working relationship between parents and teachers. Now being used successfully in educational settings across the country.
No. 050-2   **$12.95**

ASSESSMENT

CHILDREN'S ADAPTIVE BEHAVIOR SCALE (CABS)
CABS is the first of its kind—a direct assessment tool which achieves the most complete measurement of adaptive behavior available today. Designed for children aged 5 to 11; quick and easy to administer.
No. 054-5   **$19.95**

THE LOLLIPOP TEST
A Diagnostic Screening Test of School Readiness
Based on the latest research in school readiness, this culture-free test effectively measures children's readiness strengths and weaknesses. Included is all you need to give, score and interpret the test.
No. 028-6   **$19.95**

ORIENTATION TO PRESCHOOL ASSESSMENT
Combines vital child development concepts into one integrated system of child observation and assessment. This is also the user's guide to the Humanics National Child Assessment Form—Age 3 to 6.
No. 020-0   **$14.95**

ORIENTATION TO INFANT & TODDLER ASSESSMENT
User's guide to the Humanics National Child Assessment Form—Age 0 to 3. Integrates critical concepts of child development into one effective system of observation and assessment.
No. 064-2   **$14.95**

SOCIAL SERVICES

HUMANICS LIMITED SYSTEM FOR RECORD KEEPING
Designed to meet <u>all</u> record keeping needs of family oriented social service agencies, this guide integrates the child, family, social worker and community into one coherent network. Also the user's guide to proper use of Humanics Limited Record Keeping forms.
No. 027-8   **$12.95**

REAL TALK:
Exercises in Friendship and Helping Skills
Real Talk teaches students basic skills in interpersonal relationships through such methods as role-playing and modeling. An ideal human relations course for elementary, junior high and high schools.

Teacher's Manual	No. 026-X	$ 7.95
Student's Manual	No. 025-1	$12.95

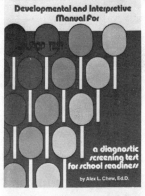

HUMANICS LIMITED

P.O. Box 7447
Atlanta, Georgia 30309
(404) 874-2176

HUMANICS LIMITED

ORDER FORM

HUMANICS LIMITED
P.O. BOX 7447/Atlanta, Georgia 30309

FOR FAST SERVICE
CALL COLLECT (404) 874-2176

QUANTITY ORDERED	ORDER NO.	BOOK TITLE	UNIT PRICE	TOTAL PRICE

☐ Payment Enclosed

☐ Institutional Purchase Order No. _____

☐ Bill my Credit Card

WHEN USING A CREDIT CARD, PLEASE CHECK PROPER BOX AND GIVE APPROPRIATE CARD AND NUMBER INFORMATION.

MASTER CARD ☐   VISA ☐

Credit Card No. ☐☐☐☐☐☐☐☐☐☐☐☐☐☐☐☐

Master Card Interbank No. ☐☐☐☐   Exp. Date month/year ☐☐☐☐

Authorized Signature (Order must be signed) _____

PLEASE TYPE, OR PRINT CLEARLY.

Subtotal	
Georgia residents add 4% sales tax	
Add shipping and handling charges	
TOTAL ORDER	

SHIP TO:

NAME_____

ADDRESS_____

CITY/STATE _____ ZIP _____

Shipping and Handling Charges

Up to $10.00 add	$1.60
$10.01 to $20.00 add	$2.60
$20.01 to $40.00 add	$3.60
$40.01 to $70.00 add	$4.60
$70.01 to $100.00 add	$5.60
$100.01 to $125.00 add	$6.60
$125.01 to $150.00 add	$7.60
$150.01 to $175.00 add	$8.60
$175.01 to $200.00 add	$9.60

Orders over $200 vary depending on method of shipment.